Anonymous

**Works on New South Wales**

Anonymous

**Works on New South Wales**

ISBN/EAN: 9783337323431

Printed in Europe, USA, Canada, Australia, Japan

Cover: Foto ©ninafisch / pixelio.de

More available books at **www.hansebooks.com**

# WORKS ON NEW SOUTH WALES.

COMPILED AT THE FREE PUBLIC LIBRARY, SYDNEY,

UNDER THE DIRECTION OF

R. C. WALKER,
PRINCIPAL LIBRARIAN.

SYDNEY: THOMAS RICHARDS, GOVERNMENT PRINTER.

1878.

4t 17—77     [1s.]

# WORKS ON NEW SOUTH WALES, RELATING TO THE FOLLOWING SUBJECTS, viz. :—

1. GEOGRAPHY OF NEW SOUTH WALES—

    NATURAL.

    ADMINISTRATIVE OR POLITICAL.

2. CLIMATE.

3. TRADE, AGRICULTURE, AND PRODUCTIONS.

4. INHABITANTS : CHARACTER, PURSUITS, LANGUAGES.

5. HISTORICAL.

6. INTERNAL ADMINISTRATION.

7. FINANCE.

8. MONEYS, WEIGHTS AND MEASURES.

NOTE.—Special information on any of the above subjects, contained in the Text, is shown by a corresponding numeral.

# WORKS ON NEW SOUTH WALES.

| Mode of Reference. | Full Title, &c. | Remarks. |
|---|---|---|
| Aborigines ... (4) | Plan to ameliorate the condition of the Aboriginal inhabitants and prevent their extermination. Sydney, 1839. 4to. Pamph. pp. 4. | Refers to the few attempts which have been made to improve the condition of the Aborigines, and to their rapid decrease. |
| Aborigines ... (4) | Aborigines — Extracts from the Papers and Proceedings of the Aborigines' Protection Society. London, 1841. 8vo. Pamph. pp. 176 | Portions of these extracts give very interesting accounts of the Aborigines of Australia. |
| Aborigines ... (4) | Report of the Parliamentary Select Committee on Aboriginal Tribes, by the Aborigines Protection Society. London, 1837. 8vo. Pamph. pp. 140. | Contains a chapter on the relations between Europeans and the Aboriginal natives of Australia. |
| Aborigines ... (4.5) | The Colonial Intelligencer, or Aborigines' Friend — Comprising the Transactions of the Aborigines Protection Society. London, 1850. 3 vols. 8vo. | Contains statements relative to the Aboriginal tribes of Australia and the conduct of the whites towards them. |
| Addison ...... (1.5) | Balmain; its Municipality and institutions. By G. R. Addison. Sydney, 1875. 12mo. Pamph. pp. 24 | Refers to a suburb of Sydney, its financial and sanitary condition, &c. |
| Agricultural Company. (3.5) | Australian Agricultural Company. Reports, 1834–40. London. 8vo. Pamphs. | This Company received a grant of 1,000,000 acres, extending from Port Stephens to the Hastings River; also valuable concessions in reference to Coal Mines at Newcastle. Subjects: Importation and increase of stock; Aborigines; Report on the land and minerals. |
| Agricultural Society. (3.5) | Anniversary Addresses (by the President); List of Members, and Rules and Regulations of the Agricultural Society of New South Wales. Sydney, 1823–26. 8vo. Pamphs. | Instituted on the 5th July, 1822. These reports give many statements of importance, and show the rapid increase of the agricultural wealth of the Colony, &c. |
| Allen ......... (3) | Lecture on Protection — Political Economy proper for New South Wales. By W. B. Allen. Sydney. (n. d.) 12mo. Pamph. pp. 24. | Favourable to protective duties on all articles introduced from abroad which can be produced in the Colony. |
| Allen ......... (1) | Journal of an Experimental Trip by the "Lady Augusta" S.S. on the River Murray. By James Allen, jun. Adelaide, 1853. 8vo., pp. 86 Pamph. | An account of the exploration of a portion of the Murray, Darling, and Murrumbidgee Rivers. |

| Mode of Reference. | Full Title, &c. | Remarks. |
|---|---|---|
| Allwood ...... (4) | Lectures on the Papal Claim of Jurisdiction, delivered before the Members of the Church of England Book Society. May and June, 1843. Sydney. 8vo. | Religious controversy. |
| Angas ......... (1.4) | Savage Life and Scenes in Australia and New - Zealand. By George French Angas. London, 1847. 2 vols. 8vo. | The small portion of the second volume which relates to New South Wales, gives a truthful picture of the habits and manners of the aboriginal inhabitants, with a description of Sydney and the Illawarra District. |
| Arden ......... (1.4) | Arden's Sydney Magazine of Politics and General Literature. Sydney, 1843. 8vo. | Contains a political Essay on New South Wales; a Satire on Colonial Society, and a Biographical Memoir of Wentworth and other representatives of the people, besides a variety of other interesting articles. |
| "Aristides"... (1.5) | Approaching Crisis of Britain and Australia. By "Aristides." Melbourne, 1854. 8vo. | A collection of letters on matters relating to the Colony, specially advocating the formation of the Riverina Territory into a separate Colony, to be called "Albertonia.". |
| Arthur ...... (1.6) | Observations upon Secondary Punishments. By Col. George Arthur. To which is added a letter on the same subject by the Archdeacon of New South Wales. Hobart Town, 1833. 8vo. Pamph. pp. 111. | The writer advocates transportation and assignment of convicts, rather than imprisonment. |
| Atkinson...... (4) | Cowandra. The Veteran's Grant. By the Authoress of Gertrude. (Miss Atkinson.) Sydney, 1859. 12mo. | Short but entertaining story of life in Australia. |
| Atkinson ...... (4) | Gertrude, the Emigrant: a Tale of Colonial Life, by an Australian Lady. (Miss Atkinson.) Sydney, 1857. Roy. 8vo. | A faithful delineation of Australian bush life. |
| Atkinson ...... (3) | On the expediency and necessity of encouraging Distilling and Brewing from Grain in New South Wales. By James Atkinson, Esq. Sydney, 1829. 8vo. Pamph. pp. 33. | A paper on general Agriculture, with special reference to the cultivation of Barley for malting. |
| Australia ...... (4.5) | Australia—An appeal to the World on behalf of the younger branch of the family of Shem. Sydney, 1839. 8vo. Pamph. pp. 88. | A protest against the outrages practised by some of the early settlers upon the Aborigines; together with a glance at their manners and language. |
| Australia ...... (3 to 6) | The Resources of Australia, and the prospects and capabilities of the New Settlement, &c., and remarks on the internal Government of New South Wales. London, 1841. 12mo. | Gives a short account of the resources and capabilities of the Colony, its internal administration, &c., at that date. |

| Mode of Reference. | Full Title, &c. | Remarks. |
|---|---|---|
| Australia...... (1.3.4) | Twenty years experience in Australia, being the evidence of disinterested and respectable residents of those Colonies, as to their present state and future prospects. London, 1839. 12mo. | A compilation from Statistical Reports and official documents, with extracts from letters, &c. |
| Australia...... (1 to 6) | The picture of Australia, exhibiting New Holland, Van Diemen's Land, and all the settlements, from the first at Sydney to the last at Swan River. London, 1829. 12mo. | Gives a general·description of the Colony, climate, soil, minerals, plants, native population, &c. |
| Australia...... (3) - | Australia, as it is. Bristol, 1840. 12mo. Pamph. pp. 48. | Statistics to 1833. A faithful representation of the prospects and resources of the Colony, with hints to immigrants. |
| Australian League. (4.5) | Sessional Papers, &c., &c., of the Australian League Conference held in Hobart Town and Launceston, Van Diemen's Land. Tasmania, 1852. 8vo. Pamph. pp. 45. | This Association was formed in the year 1851, to secure the Colony against the continuance of Transportation. |
| Australian Medical Journal. (4) | Australian Medical Journal. Sydney. 1846. 4to. | Refers almost entirely to the local practice of Medicine and Surgery. |
| Australian Museum (3) | Guide to the contents of the Australian Museum. Sydney, 1873. 8vo. Pamph. pp. 16. | Refers to a great number of specimens of the natural productions of the Colony. |
| Australian Patriotic Association (1.3.4) | A Letter from the Australian Patriotic Association to C. Buller, junr., Esq., M.P., in reply to his communication of 31st May, 1840. Sydney. 8vo. Pamph. pp. 18. | Condemns the withholding Free Institutions from New South Wales, and advocates a continuance of transportation to a limited extent, and the assignment of convicts. |
| Australian Settler's Handbook (3) | Australian Settler's Handbook. Sydney, 1861. 12mo. | Relates to the cultivation of land and management of farms in the Colony. |
| Backhouse ... (3.4.5) | A narrative of a Visit to the Australian Colonies. By James Backhouse. London, 1843. 8vo. | Contains trustworthy information relative to the state of the Colony about the year 1838, its inhabitants, productions, &c. |
| Backhouse ... (4) | Extracts from the Letters of James Backhouse, now engaged on a Missionary Visit to Van Diemen's Land and New South Wales. London, 1838. 8vo. | Describes the religious and social condition of New South Wales in 1838. |
| Badham ...... (4) | An Address to the University Debating Society. By Charles Badham, D.D. Sydney, 1875. 8vo. Pamph. pp. 13. | Inaugural Address by Professor Badham, upon the formation of the Society by members of the Sydney University. |

| Mode of Reference. | Full Title, &c. | Remarks. |
|---|---|---|
| Badham ...... (4.5) | Primary Education. By Charles Badham, D.D., Sydney, 1876. 8vo. Pamph. 14 pp. | In the form of a letter to Mr. Dalley. It disapproves of the closing of the Denominational Schools altogether, as being unfair both to Roman Catholics and Anglicans. |
| Baillierc ...... (1) | Baillierc's New South Wales Gazetteer and Road Guide. Sydney, 1866. 8vo. | Contains recent and accurate information as to all places in the Colony. |
| Baird ......... (1 to 7) | The Emigrant's Guide to Australasia. By the Rev. James Baird. London, 1868. 12mo. | A short, but correct and unbiassed description of New South Wales and adjoining Colonies. |
| Baker ......... (2.3.4) | Sydney and Melbourne, with remarks on the present state and future prospects of New South Wales. By C. J. Baker. London, 1845. 12mo. | Contains accurate and useful information on the climate and resources of the Colony; also on the state of Society in Sydney about 1842. |
| Balcombe ... (4) | Gold Pen and Pencil Sketches, or the adventures of Mr. John Slasher at the Turon Diggings. By G. F. P. (Pickering), with Illustrations by T. Balcombe. Sydney, 1852. 8vo. | A humourous account, descriptive of life at the diggings. |
| Balfour ...... (2.3) | A Sketch of New South Wales. By J. O. Balfour. London, 1845. 12mo. | Contains some useful information on the climate of New South Wales; products, sheep-farming, &c. |
| Bannister ... (4.5) | On abolishing Transportation, and on reforming the Colonial Office, in a letter to Lord John Russell. By S. Bannister, late Attorney General of New South Wales. London, 1837. 8vo. Pamph. pp. 88. | Reviews the Military system of 1792. Abuses of Colonial Government. Severity of General Darling, the Iron Collars, the Press, etc. Evil of Convict System, Remedies, Justice, Female Immigration. |
| Barrington ... (4.5) | The History of New South Wales. By Geo. Barrington. London, 1802. 8vo. A Voyage to Botany Bay, with a description of the Country, &c. By the celebrated George Barrington. London, 1794. 12mo. An Account of a Voyage to New South Wales. By George Barrington. London, 1803. 8vo. | Written by the notorious "pickpocket" B. Contains curious information on old matters of Colonial History; and gives, on the whole, a correct account of the manners and customs of the aboriginal inhabitants. |
| Barrow ...... (5) | The eventful history of the Mutiny and Piratical Seizure of H.M.S. "Bounty," its cause and consequence. By Sir John Barrow. London, 1835. 18mo. | Captain Bligh (q.v.), the Commander of "Bounty," was for a short time Governor of New South Wales. |
| Bartlett ...... (2.3.4) | New Holland, its Colonization, Productions, and Resources. By Thomas Bartlett. London, 1843. 12mo. | Gives a good deal of information as to farming, and disposal of labour; also on the natural productions and climate of New South Wales. |

| Mode of Reference. | Full Title, &c. | Remarks. |
|---|---|---|
| Barton.......... (4.5) | Report of a Trial promoted by Sir W. E. Parry, of the Australian Agricultural Company v. Accountant. By W. Barton, Esq. London, 1832. 8vo. Pamph. pp. 57. | A record of the manner in which justice was administered in the early days of the Colony. |
| Barton ...... (3.4.7) | Particulars of Joint Stock Institutions in New South Wales, with the interest that has been derived, etc., from the investment of money in that Colony. By W. Barton. Sydney, 1838. 8vo. Pamph., pp. 15. | A letter written at the instance of a capitalist, giving valuable information as to dividends paid by Public Companies at that date. |
| Barton.......... (4.5) | Literature in New South Wales. By G. B. Barton. Sydney, 1866. 8vo. | As a whole this volume constitutes a valuable contribution to the literary history of the Colony. |
| Barton.......... (4.5) | The Poets and Prose Writers of New South Wales. Edited by G. B. Barton. Sydney, 1866. 8vo. | This work throws much light on the progress of literature in the Colony. Contains extracts from the writings of some of the most prominent of Australian authors. |
| Basch ......... (1) | Atlas of the settled Counties of New South Wales. Published by Basch & Co. Sydney, 1870. Fol. | This excellent Atlas contains twenty separate maps of the counties of New South Wales, with geographical and geological information. |
| Bate........... (2.3) | Silk Cultivation. By John M. Bate. Sydney, 1864. 8vo. Pamph. pp. 16. | Showing the advantages and "adaptability of the climate" of New South Wales for the production of silk. |
| Beit........... (4.5) | Proposal for procuring German Immigrants. By J. M. Beit. Sydney, 1847. Fol. Pamph. pp. 3. | Mr. Beit suggests that £12,000 be set apart by Government to secure a full supply of immigrants from Germany. |
| Beit........... (3) | On the Management of Gold Fields. Sydney, 1851. Fol. | A letter written by Mr. Beit to the Chairman of the Committee of the Legislative Council on the management of Gold Fields, suggesting modes of obtaining revenue. |
| Belcher ...... (5) | The Mutineers of the "Bounty," and their descendants in Pitcairn and Norfolk Islands. By Lady Belcher. London, 1870. 12mo. | Norfolk Island is under the superintendence of the Governor of New South Wales. Lady Belcher's account of the islanders is most interesting. |
| Bell........... (3.7) | Industry and commerce relieved and increased by means of Free Trade and direct taxation. By Fred. A. Bell, Esq. Sydney, 1866. 8vo. Pamph. pp. 67. | Proposes to make Sydney a free port, and to adopt direct taxation, "by raising the greatest amount of the State revenue from real property, income, and house taxes." |
| Benevolent Society...... (4.5) | Reports of the Committee of the New South Wales Benevolent Society, from 1820 to 1867. Sydney. 12mo. Pamphs. | This Society was inaugurated about the year 1818, and has enjoyed the continued support of the public. Its funds are derived from private subscriptions and a Government vote. |

| Mode of Reference. | Full Title, &c. | Remarks. |
|---|---|---|
| Bennett ...... (3) | Gatherings of a Naturalist in Australia. By Geo. Bennett, F.L.S., &c. London, 1860. 8vo. | Contains interesting information on the Fauna and Flora of New South Wales. |
| Bennett ...... (3.4) | Wanderings in New South Wales, &c., during 1832–34. By George Bennett, M.D., F.L.S., &c. London, 1834. 2 vols. 8vo. | The first volume gives a very correct description of several parts of the Colony, and presents many objects of natural history, and traits of social peculiarity. |
| Bennett ...... (1.5) | The History of Australian Discovery and Colonization. By Samuel Bennett. Sydney, 1866. 8vo. | "The history of the Colony has been brought down to the administration of Governor Darling, which lasted from 1825 to 1831. In more than one respect this is the best of our historical productions." — *Barton's Literature in N.S.W.* |
| Bentham ...... (3) | Flora Australiensis; a description of the Plants of the Australian Territory. By George Bentham, F.R.S., &c., assisted by Ferdinand Mueller, M.D., &c. London, 1863–73. 6 vols., 8vo. | The latest and most complete work on the Botany of Australia yet published |
| Berncastle ... (1) | The defenceless state of Sydney. How it can be defended, and how it can be taken. By Dr. Berncastle. Sydney, 1865. 8vo. Pamph. pp. 34. | Suggests a mode of fortifying the harbour. |
| Beuzeville ... (3) | Practical instructions for the management of Silk-worms, according to the best methods of the breeders of the silk-growing countries, &c., adapted to New South Wales. By James Beuzeville, Sydney. 8vo. Pamph. pp. 13. | A handbook for the rearing of Silk-worms. |
| Bigge ......... (3·4) | Report of the Commissioner of Inquiry on the state of Agriculture and Trade in the Colony of New South Wales. By Thomas Bigge, C.E. London, 1823. Fol. | An accurate Report on the state of Agriculture and Trade, character of the population, &c., in the early days of the Colony. |
| Bigge ......... (4.5.6) | Report of the Commissioner of Inquiry on the Judicial Establishments of New South Wales and Van Diemen's Land. By Thomas Bigge. London, 1823. Fol. | The result of inquiries into the state of the criminal and civil judicature of the Colony. |
| Bigge ......... (4.5) | Report of the Commissioner of Inquiry on the State of the Colony of New South Wales. By Thomas Bigge. London, 1822. Fol. | This Report refers wholly to the condition, treatment, and employment of the convicts. |

| Mode of Reference. | Full Title, &c. | Remarks. |
|---|---|---|
| Bingle ......... (4.5) | Letter to the Right Hon. His Majesty's Principal Secretary of State for the Colonies, London, from John Bingle, Esq., one of His Majesty's Justices of the Peace for the Colony of New South Wales, Sydney August 15, 1832, with the Official Correspondence with the Colonial Government of that Colony. Sydney, 1832. 8vo. Pamph. pp. 40. | Has reference to the punishment by Bingle of three of his assigned servants by administering 100 lashes; and subsequent proceedings. |
| Binney......... (4) | Lights and Shadows of Church-life in Australia, including Thoughts on some Things at Home. By the Rev. T. Binney. London, 1860. 8vo. | The Rev. T. Binney visited Australia about 1860, and his book records his impressions of the religious state of the Colonies; and also contains correspondence with various Church Dignitaries. |
| Blackie ...... (1 to 6) | The Imperial Gazetteer, a General Dictionary of Geography: Physical, Political, Statistical, and Descriptive. Edited by W. G. Blackie, Ph. D. London and Edinburgh, 1855. Roy. 8vo. 2 vols. | New South Wales is the subject of a very comprehensive article, treating of its coast-line, geology, vegetation, government, etc. Sydney is fully described, and a map of the harbour is given. Large amount of information regarding the fauna and flora of the continent, under the head of Australia. |
| Bland ......... (4.5) | Services rendered to New South Wales by W. Bland. Sydney, 1862. 8vo. Pamph. pp. 15. | Refers to the attempt made by the friends of Dr. B. to obtain some recognition of his public services by the Legislature. |
| Bland ......... (5) | Letters to Chas. Buller, jr., Esq., M.P., from the Australian Patriotic Association. By W. Bland. Sydney, 1849. 8vo. | Dr. Bland was one of the most persistent exponents of the principles of the Patriotic Association. These papers are of great historic value. |
| Blaxland ...... (1) | The Journal of a Tour of Discovery across the Blue Mountains, in New South Wales. By G. Blaxland. London, 1823. 12mo. | A brief but accurate and interesting description of the interior of New South Wales. |
| Bligh ......... (5) | A Voyage to the South Seas in His Majesty's ship "Bounty," with an Account of the Mutiny on board the said ship. By W. Bligh. London, 1792. 4to. | The mutiny was occasioned by Bligh's severity; he was afterwards appointed Governor of the Colony, but was not successful in his administration. |
| Bonwick ...... (4.5) | Curious Facts of Old Colonial Days. By James Bonwick. London, 1870. 12mo. | A trustworthy book, relating principally to the social state of the Colony in primitive times. |
| Bonwick ...... (5) | Discovery and Settlement of Port Phillip, being a history of the country now called Victoria, up to the arrival of Mr. Superintendent Latrobe, in October, 1839. By James Bonwick. Melbourne, 1856. 12mo. | During the time to which the details of this volume refer, Port Phillip formed part of the Colony of New South Wales. |

| Mode of Reference. | Full Title, &c. | Remarks. |
|---|---|---|
| Botany Bay... (5) | Captain Cook landing in Botany Bay, with *Fac Simile* of Cook's Chart, and view of Monument to Captain Cook. Gibbs, Shallard, & Co. Sydney. Pamph. pp. 12. | An interesting memoir of the first Englishman who landed in New South Wales. This pamphlet was privately printed and circulated by the Hon. Thos. Holt upon the completion of the monument erected by him to the memory of the illustrious navigator. |
| Brabazon ... (3.4) | Brabazon's New South Wales General Town Directory and Advertiser. Sydney, 1848. 8vo. | In addition to the Directory, the volume contains a list of the public and private institutions of Sydney. |
| Bradshaw ... (1.3) | Bradshaw's Almanac and General Guide for 1872–76. Sydney. 8vo. | Contains a postal and road Guide, besides other useful information. |
| Brady ......... (3) | Silk. By Chas. Brady, F.L.S. Sydney, 1871. 8vo. Pamph. pp. 25. | Contains a good deal of valuable information on the production of silk in the Colony. |
| Brady ......... (3) | The Ailant Silkworm—observations on its habit, management, &c. Contributed by Charles Brady. Sydney, 1868. 8vo. Pamph. pp. 38. | Relates to the production of silk in the Colony. |
| Brady and Thorne. (3) | Silk Culture in New South Wales. By Charles Brady. Silk-growing. By Charles Thorne. Sydney, 1871. 4to. Pamph. pp. 8. | Trustworthy account of the operations and experiments carried on in the production of silk in the Colony. |
| Braim ......... (1.2.5.6.7) | History of New South Wales from its settlement to the close of the year 1844. By T. H. Braim. London, 1846. 2 vols. 8vo. | A statistical, historical, and political account of the Colony, with a brief sketch of the various administrations to about 1844. Trustworthy. |
| Breton ...... (3.4.5.) | Excursions in New South Wales, Western Australia, and Van Dieman's Land, during the years 1830 to 1833. By Lieut. Breton, R.N. London, 1833. 8vo. | Chiefly devoted to a description of the Aborigines in various parts of Australia. Has also short notes on the natural productions and early settlements of the Colony. |
| Brodribb ...... (1.2.3.6) | A plain statement of facts addressed to the small and large capitalists and the labouring classes in England and elsewhere, on the great capabilities and natural advantages of the Australian Colonies, particularly New South Wales and Victoria, for emigration. By W. A. Brodribb, Esq., a late Member of the Legislature of Victoria, and a Magistrate of twelve years standing in that province of New South Wales. London, 1862. Pamph. pp. 32. | Mr. Brodribb describes the mode of acquiring and of successfully working Station properties; and places before his readers in a clear manner the advantages which the Colonies afford to all industrious and sober men, in pastoral and agricultural pursuits. Describes the Assisted Emigration Scheme of Victoria and the Land Regulations of New South Wales. |
| Broughton ... (4.5) | A letter in vindication of the principles of the Reformation, addressed to Roger Therry, Esq., in consequence of a speech delivered by him in the Roman Catholic Chapel at Sydney, on Sunday, July 29th, 1832. By the Rev. W. Grant Broughton, M.A., Archdeacon of New South Wales and its dependencies. Sydney, 1832. pp. 27. | Religious controversy. |

| Mode of Reference. | Full Title, &c. | Remarks. |
|---|---|---|
| Broughton ... (4) | A Charge delivered to the Clergy of New South Wales, at the visitation held on Thursday, Feb. 13th, 1834, in the Church of St. James, at Sydney, by W. Grant Broughton, M.A., etc. Sydney 1834. pp. 21. | Religious. |
| Broughton ... (4) | Education : a Petition. The humble Petition of William Grant Broughton, Doctor in Divinity, Bishop and Ordinary Pastor of the Diocese of Australia. Sydney, 1836. Pamph. pp. 8. | A protest against the proposed system of general Education. |
| Broughton ... (4) | The Speech of the Bishop of Australia at the Entertainment given to His Honor Mr. Justice Burton, on his return to the Colony. 27th May, 1841. | Contains arguments in favour of extended and higher education. |
| Broughton ... (4) | The Speech of the Lord Bishop of Australia in the Legislative Council, upon the resolution for establishing a system of general Education. By the Right Rev. W. G. Broughton, D.D. Sydney, 1839. pp. 43. | The Bishop contends that education cannot be properly given without religious instruction ; and that religious instruction can only be given when the children of various denominations are separately taught. |
| Broughton ... (4) | A Speech delivered at the Committee of Protestants, on Wednesday, August 3rd, 1836, on Education, by the Bishop of Australia. Sydney, 1836. 8vo. pp. 23. | Claiming that prayer, the reading of the Bible, and religious instruction, should form part of the duties in State supported Schools. |
| Broughton ... (4.5) | Circular on Roman Catholic Interference. By the Right Rev. W. G. Broughton, D.D. Sydney, 1847. Fol. pp. 4. | The Rev. W. Bodenham reported to the Bishop that an Episcopalian, residing in his parish, being near death, was visited by a Roman Catholic priest and induced to join the Roman Catholic Church. |
| Brown ...... (3) | Prodromus Floræ Novæ Hollandiæ et Insulæ Van Diemen, exhibens characteres Plantarum, quas annis 1802-1805, per oras utriusque insulæ, collegit et descripsit Robertus Brown. Norimbergae, 1827. 8vo. Supplementum. London, 1830. 8vo. | A most important work on the Botany of New South Wales. |
| Buchanan...... (4.5) | Political Portraits of some of the Members of the Parliament of New South Wales. By David Buchanan, Esq., Sydney, 1863. 8vo. Pamph. pp. 56. | Sketches of the history and characteristics of some of the leading Public Men of the Colony. |
| Burton ...... (4.5) | The state of Religion and Education in New South Wales. By William Westbrook Burton, one of the Judges of the Supreme Court of New South Wales. London, 1840. 8vo. | A valuable authority on the social condition of the Colony. Some of the statements made gave rise to controversy. (See Ullathorne.) |

| Mode of Reference. | Full Title, &c. | Remarks. |
|---|---|---|
| Burton......... (1.3.6.7) | Visitors' Guide to Sydney ; comprising description of the City and its Institutions. By Edwin Burton. Sydney, 1874. 12mo. | An excellent and correct description of Sydney at the present time. Contains valuable statistical information. |
| Busby ......... (3.4) | Authentic Information relative to New South Wales, and New Zealand. By James Busby. London, 1832. 12mo. | Contains information for emigrants, and observations on Crown Lands, &c., to 1832. |
| Bush Mission (4) | Reports of the New South Wales Bush Missionary Society. | The Bush Missionary Society sends out itinerant missionaries and has local agents in every principal town in the Colony, now numbering about one hundred. Supported by the voluntary subscriptions of members of all Protestant denominations. |
| Butterfield ... (4) | Letters to Members, &c., of the N.S.W. Bush Missionary Society. By Joseph Palmer and G. Butterfield. Sydney, 1864. | See Bush Mission. |
| Byrne ......... (3.4) | Twelve years' wanderings in the British Colonies, 1835–47. By J. C. Byrne. London, 1848. 2 vols. 8vo. | That part which refers to New South Wales treats principally of the produce, climate, state of society, and mode of government. Some of the statements made are questionable. |
| Cameron ...... (2.3.4) | New South Wales; its progress and resources. (By A. M. Cameron.) Sydney, 1876. 8vo. | A short but correct statistical account of the Colony to the end of the year 1874. |
| Campbell...... (3) | The Crown Lands of Australia. By William Campbell. Glasgow, 1855. 8vo. | Contains information on the land regulations, and puts forth the grievances of the tenants of the Crown, and the alleged infringement of their rights. |
| Catholic Almanac. (4) | The Catholic Almanac and Directory for Divine Service in the Archdiocese of Sydney. Sydney, 1854–61. | Contains some useful statistical information. |
| "Catholicus". (4) | An original Essay on Popular Education; its general merits, and special adaptation to the circumstances of the Colony of New South Wales. By Catholicus. Sydney, 1848. 8vo. Pamph. pp. 16. | Suggests a modification of the Denominational system, and the use of the Irish School Books. |
| Chambers ... (1 to 6) | Chambers's Edinburgh Journal— Conducted by W. & R. Chambers. London, 1833–53. 12 vols., fol. | Contains several interesting and trustworthy articles on New South Wales. |
| Chambers...... (5) | Address to the People of New South Wales ; in opposition to, and refutation of the Grievance Petition of the Legislative Council to Parliament ; and displaying the impolicy of the Constitution Bills. By Chas. H. Chambers. Sydney, 1853. 8vo. Pamph. pp. 21. | In opposition to the Petition for a new Constitution. |

| Mode of Reference. | Full Title, &c. | Remarks. |
|---|---|---|
| Chambers ... (1 to 4) | Chambers's Encyclopædia; a Dictionary of universal knowledge for the People. Illustrated with Maps and numerous Wood Engravings. By W. & R. Chambers. London, 1874. 10 vols. Roy. 8vo. | Has special articles at considerable length on *Australia, Australasia, New South Wales, and Sydney;* and contains the latest statistics. |
| Chapman ... (5) | Parliamentary Government or Responsible Ministries for the Australian Colonies. By H. S. Chapman. Tasmania, 1854. 8vo. Pamph. pp. 39. | Advocates as full and complete adoption of the principles of the British Constitution as the circumstances of these Colonies will permit. |
| Chisholm...... (5) | Emigration and transportation relatively considered, in a letter dedicated by permission to Earl Grey. By Mrs. Chisholm. London, 1847. 12mo. Pamph. pp. 36. | Mrs. Chisholm recommends a liberal Emigration scheme, and urges that the difficulties in the way of emigration have caused many men to commit crimes that they might be transported, and so obtain a free passage to the Colonies. |
| Chisholm...... (5) | What has Mrs. Chisholm done for New South Wales. Sydney, 1862. 8vo. Pamph. pp. 22. | Describes Mrs. Chisholm's efforts in the cause of Immigration, and suggests that her services should be recognized and rewarded. |
| Church ...... (4.5) | The Church of England, and the Sydney University. Sydney, 1852. Kemp & Fairfax. 12mo. Pamph. pp. 70. | Documents and correspondence reprinted from the *Sydney Morning Herald,* showing the demands made by the Church of England for a voice in the affairs of the University. |
| Church ...... (4.5) | Minutes of Proceedings at a Meeting of the Metropolitan and Suffragan Bishops of the Province of Australasia, held at Sydney, 1850. 8vo. Pamph. pp. 24. | This meeting was held in consequence of doubts existing as to how far the Ecclesiastical laws of England applied to the province of Australasia. |
| Church ...... (4.5) | Report of a Committee of the Commission of the General Assembly of the Church of Scotland, relative to the division in the Presbyterian Church of New South Wales; and relative documents. Edinburgh, 1840. Pamphlet, pp. 61. Appendix, pp. 53. | Full of interesting information on the past History of the Presbyterian Church of New South Wales. |
| Church ...... (4.5) | Minutes of the Synod of Australia, in connexion with the established Church of Scotland. Sydney, 1840–1842. 8vo. Pamphlets. | Gives the names of Ministers and other information in reference to the Presbyterian Church. |
| City Mission.. (4) | Reports of the Sydney City Mission, for 1863. Sydney. 8vo. Pamph. pp. 23. | Inaugurated 1861. Funds derived from private subscription from members of all sections of Protestant Churches. |
| City Night Refuge. (4) | City Night Refuge and Soup Kitchen. Report, Sydney, 1870. 8vo. Pamph. pp. 16. | Instituted July 22nd, 1867. Upwards of 30,000 meals were given during the first year. In 1870, meals given, 70,000; night's shelter, 14,000. |

| Mode of Reference. | Full Title, &c. | Remarks. |
|---|---|---|
| Clacy ......... (4) | Lights and Shadows of Australian Life. By Mrs. Clacy. London, 1854. 2 vols. 8vo. | A novel founded on incidents of bush life in Australia. |
| Clark .. ....... (1.2.5.) | Sydney Water Supply : Report to the Government of New South Wales on various projects for supplying Sydney with water. By W. Clarke, C.E., Sydney, 1877. Fol.—Sydney Drainage : Report to the Government of New South Wales on the interception and disposal of the drainage of the City of Sydney and Suburbs. By W. Clark, C.E. Sydney, 1877. Fol. | Mr. Clark was engaged by the Agent General in England to proceed to this colony for the purpose of advising the Government on the subject of the water supply and the drainage of the City of Sydney. |
| Clarke ......... (2.3) | Effects of Forest Vegetation on Climate, by the Rev. W. B. Clarke, M.A., F.R.S., &c., &c. Sydney, 1876. 8vo. Pamph. pp. 57. | Written to prove the value of forests in conserving moisture in the soil. The disastrous results arising from indiscriminate destruction of forests proved by numerous quotations. |
| Clarke ......... (3) | Researches in the Southern Gold Fields of New South Wales. By the Rev. W. B. Clarke, M.A., &c. Sydney, 1860. 12mo. | Contains valuable facts connected with the great discovery of gold in New South Wales. |
| Clarke ......... (3) | Recent Geological Discoveries in Australasia. By the Rev. W. B. Clarke, M.A., &c. Sydney, 1861, 8vo. | Contains valuable information as to the physical structure of New South Wales. |
| Clarke ......... (5) | Santa Cruz. By the Rev. W. B. Clarke, M.A., &c. Sydney, 1875. 12mo. Pamph. pp. 10. | A short Poem, occasioned by the murder of Commodore Goodenough at Santa Cruz, a small island in the South Pacific Ocean. |
| — Clarke ......... (4) | *Sedimentary formations, N.S.W. New. ed. 1878. pp. 165 maps.* A Sermon preached in St. Thomas's Church, Willoughby, on Sunday, 27th February, 1848. By the Rev. W. B. Clarke, M.A. Sydney, 1848. 8vo. Pamph. pp. 60. | Refers to the doctrine and practices of the Roman Catholic Church. |
| Clarke ......... (5) | Sermon preached in St. Thomas's Church, Willoughby, on Sunday morning, July 10th, 1864. By the Rev. W. B. Clarke, M.A. Sydney, 1864. 8vo. Pamph. pp. 16. | Preached in aid of funds for the relief of sufferers by the floods in the agricultural districts of the Colony. |
| Clarke ......... (4) | A Sermon preached in the Church of St. James, Sydney, on Thursday 24th June, 1840. By the Rev. W. B. Clarke, M.A., Sydney, 1840. 8vo. Pamph. pp. 20. | Preached at the Anniversary of the Diocesan Committee of the Societies for the Propagation of the Gospel in foreign parts, and for promoting Christian knowledge. |
| Cockburn....... (4) | General Education considered with reference to the antagonistic bearings on it of the principles of the National System, defined as Socialism, Socinianism, and Infidelity. By H. N. Cockburn. Sydney, 1859. 8vo. Pamph. pp. 26. | Enunciates the views of those favourable to Denominational Education, asserts that it is the duty of Government to assist education, but not to control it, and that education is not the province of the Clergy. |

| Mode of Reference. | Full Title, &c. | Remarks. |
|---|---|---|
| Cockerell ...... (4.5) | Scenes behind the Curtain, or acts and deeds of the Convict Detectives of New South Wales, as illustrated in the Trial which led to the conviction of John Cockerell. By J. T. Cockerell. Brisbane, 1861. Pamph. pp. 50. | Cockerell was convicted of unlawful practices in connection with his business as pawnbroker, and exposes the conduct of those who prosecuted him. |
| Collins ......... (1.2.4.5) | An account of the English Colony of New South Wales. Compiled from the MSS. of Lieut.-Governor King. By David Collins. London. 1798-1802. 2 vols. 4to. | A detailed, and without doubt, faithful account, of events from the foundation of the Colony to the end of the year 1800. |
| Colman ...... (3) | The New South Wales Almanac and Remembrancer for 1848. Published by W. A. Colman. Sydney. 12mo. | Full of statistical information. |
| Colonization .. (5) | The debate upon Mr. Ward's resolutions on Colonization in the House of Commons, June 27th, 1839, containing the speeches of H. G. Ward, Esq., M.P., Sir William Molesworth, Bart., M.P., and others. London, 1839. 8vo. Pamph., pp. 84. | These speeches deserve careful consideration, though they refer to an epoch in the Colony's history which has passed away. |
| Commerce ... (3.4.7) | Commerce and Finance of Australia. London, 1856. 12mo., pp. 51. | Especial reference to the Banking Statistics of Australia and the Securities issued by the respective Governments. |
| Connell ...... (6) | The New South Wales Magisterial Digest. By H. Connell. Sydney, 1866. 8vo. | A valuable legal work. |
| Constitution... (5) | The New Constitution. A letter to Henry Parkes, Esq. By Conservative Squaretoes. Sydney, 1852. pp. 14. | Objections to a proposal to form the Upper House from Members who had been previously elected as Members of the Council ; suggests that the Upper House should consist of 21 Members, viz. :—7 Official Members of the Government, and 14 nominated by the Governor for life. |
| Constitution... (5) | Observations on the proposed New Constitution for New South Wales. By an Old Colonist. Sydney, 1852. Pamph. pp. 16. | On the effect, influence, and composition of an Upper House for the Colony. |
| Convict Barracks. (5) | Government and General Orders, dated 1st May, 1819, relative to the Convict Barracks. Sydney, 1819. 16mo. Pamph. pp. 17. | The Barracks were erected for the accommodation of those convicts in the immediate service of the Government. |
| Cook ......... (5) | The Three Voyages of Captain James Cook round the World. London, 1821. 7 vols. 8vo. | Contains account of the discovery of New South Wales by Captain Cook, and his landing at Botany Bay, April, 1770. |
| Corbyn ...... (4) | Sydney Revels of Bacchus, Cupid, and Momus, etc. By C. A. Corbyn. Sydney, 1854. 8vo. | Chiefly consists of amusing incidents derived from Police and Law Reports. |

B

| Mode of Reference. | Full Title, &c. | Remarks. |
|---|---|---|
| Council of Education. (4) | Reports of the Council of Education upon the condition of Public Schools. Sydney, 1867–76. Fol. | Very valuable information on social and educational matters. |
| Cox ............ (3) | A Monograph of Australian Land Shells. By James C. Cox, M.D., &c. Sydney, 1868. 8vo. | Valuable contributions to the study of Conchology. |
| Cox ............ (4) | Catalogue of Specimens of the Australian Land Shells, in the collection of James C. Cox, M.D., &c. Sydney, 1864. 12mo. | |
| Cox & Co...... (3) | Cox & Co.'s Sydney Post Office Directory for 1857. Sydney. 8vo. | Contains but little information that is likely to be useful at the present day. |
| Croker ......... (4.5) | Memoirs of Joseph Holt. Edited by T. Crofton Croker. London, 1838. 2 vols. 8vo. | Gives a curious and interesting account of New South Wales from about 1800 to 1812. Some of the statements made are questionable. |
| Cunningham.. (1 to 5) | Two Years in New South Wales. By Peter Cunningham, R.N. London, 1827. 2 vols. 12mo. | An excellent book of general information on the Colony. Dates from 1824 to 1826. |
| Cunningham.. (3) | Hints for Australian Emigrants. By Peter Cunningham. London, 1841. 8vo. | Contains observations on Australian grasses, methods of irrigation, &c. |
| Darling ...... (5) | Governor Darling's refutation of the charges of cruelty and oppression of the soldiers Sudds and Thompson, at Sydney, N.S.W., Nov., 1826. By Miles. London, 1832. pp. 32. | Two soldiers committed a robbery in Sydney, and being convicted, were loaded with chains and iron-spiked collars of peculiar construction, which were said to have caused Sudds's death. |
| Darling ...... (5) | Debates in the House of Commons during the Session of 1835 upon Mr. Maurice O'Connell's motion for a Select Committee to inquire into the conduct of General Darling whilst Governor of New South Wales; also the case of Captain Robison. London, 1835. Pamph. pp. 78. | (See " Robison.") |
| Darling ...... (5) | Letter addressed by Lieut.-Gen. R. Darling, late Governor of New South Wales, to Joseph Hume, Esq., M.P. London, 1832. 8vo. Pamph. pp. 48. | In refutation of charges of mal-administration and oppression brought against the Governor by Messrs. Hall and Hume. |
| Darwin ...... (1.4) | Narrative of the Surveying Voyages in His Majesty's ships "Adventure" and "Beagle" between 1826 and 1836. Journal and Remarks; by C. Darwin. London, 1839. 3 vols. 8vo. | Chap. 21, vol. 3, is devoted to a description of Sydney, a trip over the Blue Mountains, and a short reference to social matters. |
| Davison ...... (3) | The Discovery and Geognosy of Gold Deposits in Australia, &c. By Simpson Davison. London, 1860. 8vo. | Refers to the discovery of gold, the state of the gold-fields, and gives various papers and reports on the Aurageology of New South Wales. |

| Mode of Reference. | Full Title, &c. | Remarks. |
|---|---|---|
| Dawson ...... (4.5) | Present state of Australia, 1830–31. By R. Dawson. London, 1831. 8vo. | Contains an excellent and correct description of the manners and customs of the Aboriginal inhabitants. |
| Do Boos ...... (4) | Fifty Years ago. An Australian Tale, by Chas. De Boos. Sydney, 1867. 8vo. | Portraying the peculiarities of our bush population, their modes of thought and expression. |
| Denichy ...... (5) | How I became Attorney General of New Barataria. By D. H. Denichy. Sydney, 1860. 12mo. Pamph. pp. 24. | A satire on an incident in political affairs. |
| Denison ...... (4.5) | Varieties of Vice-regal Life. By Sir William Denison, K.C.B. London, 1870. 2 vols. 8vo. | A considerable portion of the first volume is devoted almost exclusively to New South Wales, and is full of interesting information on almost every topic. |
| Derwent Star (5) | The Derwent Star and Van Diemen's Land Intelligencer. Hobart Town, Tuesday, April 3rd, 1810. Fol. (A reprint.) | Contains an account of the death and obsequies of Lieut.-Governor Collins. |
| Destitute Children. (4) | Society for the Relief of Destitute Children, Randwick. Reports. Sydney, 1853–71. 8vo. | This is an important institution, supported by Government grants and voluntary contributions. |
| Dickinson ... (5) | A letter to the Honorable the Speaker of the Legislative Council on the formation of a Second Chamber in the Legislature of New South Wales. By John Nodes Dickinson, Esq., one of the Judges of the Supreme Court. Sydney, 1852. 8vo. Pamph. pp. 32. | Proposes the creation of a Baronetage for New South Wales ; the dignity to be conferred on every fit and proper person who shall purchase a certain quantity of land, and settle a number of married couples as tenants upon it ; the upper House to be formed by election, either by the people or by Parliament, of the required number of Baronets. |
| Dobson ...... (2) | Australian Cyclonology, or the Law of Storms in the South Pacific Ocean and on the Coasts of Australia, Tasmania, New Zealand, etc., etc. By Thomas Dobson, B.A. Tasmania, 1853. 8vo. Pamph. pp. 103. | Mr. Dobson has collected an immense amount of data on the subject of wind currents and hurricanes, and his deductions therefrom appear to have been carefully prepared. |
| Donnison...... (4.5) | The Brisbane Water Cases. Being a narrative of the Trials of Messrs. Bean, Donnison, and Moore, and their respective actions against Captain Faunce; illustrated with a few remarks on the Government of Sir Richard Bourke, etc. By H. Donnison. Sydney, 1838. 8vo. Pamph. pp. 89. | Discloses a lax state of law, and various corrupt practices, which have long since ceased in the Colony. |
| Drought ...... (5) | A Form of Prayer with Thanksgiving to be used on Thursday, Nov. 12th, 1829, in all Churches and Chapels of the Establishment throughout New South Wales, in acknowledgment of the mercy of God in putting an end to the late severe drought, etc. By special command of His Excellency the Governor. Sydney, 1829. pp. 9. | Commemorating the close of a long continued and disastrous drought. |

| Mode of Reference. | Full Title, &c. | Remarks. |
|---|---|---|
| Duncan ...... (5) | Duncan's Weekly Register of Politics, Facts and General Literature. Sydney, 1843–45. 4to. | This journal, which reached only its 127th number, contains many able articles, written during a period of almost unexampled commercial depression. |
| Duncan ...... (5) | A plea for the New South Wales Constitution. By W. A. Duncan. Sydney, 1856. 8vo. Pamph. pp. 23. | In favour of the present Constitution of the Colony. |
| Duncan.. ........ (4) | Lecture on National Education: delivered at the School of Arts, Brisbane. By W. A. Duncan, Esq. Brisbane, 1850. 8vo. Pamph. pp. 23. | Favourable to the National System as opposed to the Denominational. |
| Duncan........ (4.5) | A letter to the Lord Bishop of Australia, containing remarks upon His Lordship's protest against the Metropolitan and Episcopal Jurisdiction of His Grace the Archbishop of Sydney. By W. A. Duncan. Sydney, 1843. 8vo. Pamph. pp. 24. | Controversial (religious). |
| Duncan........ (4.5) | A second letter to the Lord Bishop of Australia, in reply to the Lectures of the Rev. R. Allwood, B.A., Minister of St. James's, against the Bishop of Rome's Supremacy. By W. A. Duncan. Sydney, 1843. 8vo. Pamph. pp. 40. | Controversy between Protestants and Catholics in reference to Papal Supremacy. (See Allwood.) |
| Duncan........ (4) | On Self-supporting Agricultural Working Unions for the Labouring Classes. By W. A. Duncan. Sydney, 1844. 8vo. Pamph. pp. 16. | Agricultural Unions recommended. |
| Duncan........ (5) | Account of a Memorial presented to His Majesty by Captain Pedro Fernandez de Quir, concerning the population and discovery of the fourth part of the world, Australia the Unknown. From the Spanish, with an introductory Notice, by W. A. Duncan, Esq. Sydney, 1874. 8vo. | A curious account of the supposed discovery of Australia by De Quiros in 1610. |
| Dyer .......... (1 to 7) | The Sydney Magazine of Science and Art. Edited by Joseph Dyer. Sydney, 1858–59. 8vo. | Contains a large amount of valuable information on nearly all topics relating to New South Wales. |
| Eagar.......... (5.7) | Financial Statement: Speech of the Hon. Geoffrey Eagar, Colonial Treasurer, in moving the first resolution in Committee of Ways and Means, in the Legislative Assembly, on Thursday, the 27th September, 1866. 8vo. Pamph. pp. 39, and Appendix. | Throws a good deal of light on the state of the Colony, financially, about the year 1866. Appended is given an "outline of a project for the establishment of a National Bank." |

| Mode of Reference. | Full Title, &c. | Remarks. |
|---|---|---|
| Earl .......... (1) | Contributions to the Physical Geography of South-eastern Asia and Australia. By George Windsor Earl, M.R.A.S. London, 1853. 8vo. Pamph. pp. 48. | A valuable treatise on the relation of Australia to the neighbouring islands, as shown by its physical character and the range of some of its plants and animals. |
| Earl ... ........ (5) | The Steam Route from Singapore to Sydney, via Torres Straits. By G. W. Earl. Reprinted from the "Nautical Magazine." London. (n.d.) 8vo. Pamph. pp. 20. | Recommending the Torres Strait route for Mail service. |
| Eden .......... (3.4.5) | The History of New Holland, from its discovery in 1616 to the present time. By the Right Hon. W. Eden. London, 1787. 8vo. | Written by Lord Auckland ; gives a short but correct history of the discovery of New South Wales, with an account of its products and inhabitants. |
| Education .... (4.5) | Public Education. Regulations issued from the Colonial Secretary's Office, Sydney, 24th September, 1841. 12mo. pp. 4. | Defines the manner in which aid will be afforded by Government to Public Schools. |
| Education .... (4.5) | Minutes of His Excellency Sir Richard Bourke to the Legislative Council, Sydney, 1836. Fol. | With reference to one day in the week besides Sunday being set apart for religious instruction in schools. |
| Education .... (4.5) | Concise statement of the principles of the British and Foreign School Society; with a sketch of the Society's history and system of teaching. By the Australian School Society. Sydney, 1839. 8vo. Pamph. pp. 60. | Refers to the Society's system of religious instruction. |
| Education .... (4.5) | Statement explanatory of the System of Education administered by the National Board of New South Wales. Sydney, 1858. 8vo. Pamph. pp. 22. | Contents : Establishment of schools ; teachers ; list. of books sanctioned by the Commissioners ; government of schools ; conduct of schools ; daily routine ; time-table ; non-vested schools. |
| Education ... (4.5) | The Protestant Proceedings Vindicated from the imputation of political faction, etc.; being the substance of a Speech delivered at the General Committee of Protestants. Sydney, 1836. 8vo. Pamph. pp. 8. | Opposed to the Irish System of National Education, as being "subversive of the fundamental principle of Protestantism," and advocates, in any system of Education which the State may provide, the free and unrestricted use of the Holy Scriptures. |
| Education ... (4.5) | General Education Vindicated; being the Report from the Select Committee on Education, etc. The Report of the Public Meeting at the School of Arts, on Saturday, Sept. 7th, etc., etc., etc. Sydney, 1844. 8vo. Pamph. pp. 64. | In favour of Lord Stanley's System of Education as a basis for general Education in this Colony. |
| Education ... (4.5) | National Education : a series of letters in defence of the National System, against the attacks of an anonymous writer in the Sydney Morning Herald. By the Teachers of the National Schools of Sydney. 1857. 8vo. Pamph. pp. 48. | The principal points these letters endeavour to prove are—That the National System is not expensive ; that it is popular among all classes of the community ; that it has made satisfactory progress, and is exactly suited to the wants of the Colony ; that the National System is fully as religious as the Denominational, &c., &c. |

| Mode of Reference. | Full Title, &c. | Remarks. |
|---|---|---|
| Education ... (4.5) | General Education. The Protestant Resolutions and Petitions to His Excellency the Governor, Sir R. Bourke. Sydney, June 24th, 1836. Fol. Pamph. pp. 6. | In favour of a system of Education combining religious instruction with the general course of lessons. |
| Eipper......... (4) | Statement of the Origin, Condition, and Prospects of the German Mission to the Aborigines at Moreton Bay. By the Rev. C. Eipper. Sydney, 1841. 8vo. Pamph. pp. 16 | Conducted under the auspices of the Presbyterian (Dr. Lang's) Church. An interesting account of the Aborigines, with short vocabulary of their language. |
| Emigration ... (4) | Direct remission advocated ; being a consideration of the connection between the Waste Lands of the Colonies and Emigration. Sydney, 1848. pp. 20. | "Well worthy of perusal, and throws out one of the most valuable suggestions on the subject of Emigration," viz., a proposal to issue to Emigrants "Land Scrip to represent average cost of passage." (*Sydney Morning Herald.*) See also Immigration. |
| Encyclopædia (1.3.4) | Encyclopædia Britannica ; or, Dictionary of Arts, Sciences, and General Literature. 7th edition. Adam and Chas. Black. Edinburgh, 1842. 24 vols. 4to. | Contains interesting and truthful description of Sydney up to 1836. All the Colonies of Australia are included under the general head Australasia, and the notices are brief. |
| Entomological Society. (3) | Transactions of the Entomological Society of New South Wales. Sydney, 1862-73. 8vo. | Refers to the structure, uses, habits, and functions of the insect tribes found in New South Wales and other parts of Australia. |
| Fairfax ...... (1) | Handbook of Australasia. By W. Fairfax. Melbourne, 1859. 12mo. | A useful work of reference, and contains a list of works on Australia. |
| Farrer ......... (3) | Grass and Sheep Farming : a Paper, speculative and suggestive. By William Farrer, B.A. Sydney, 1873. 8vo. | Contains useful observations on the pastoral resources of the Colony, its Land Law, &c. |
| Field ......... (1.3) | Geographical Memoirs of New South Wales. By Barron Field, F.L.S. London, 1825. 8vo. | An interesting work. Contains some valuable papers on the Geography, Geology, &c. of the Colony, by other authors. The information respecting the rivers of New South Wales is trustworthy. |
| Fisher ......... (4) | Colonial Law Reform. By T. J. Fisher, Barrister-at-law. Sydney, 1870. 8vo. Pamph. pp. 27. | Refers to the Draft Colonial Law Reform Act of 1869, the ends in view being—"the facilitating, simplifying, cheapening, and expediting the administration of justice in the Supreme Court of the Colony." |
| Fitzgerald ... (3) | Australian Orchids. By R. D. Fitzgerald, F.L.S. Sydney, 1876-77. Parts 1—3. Atlas folio. | A work of great merit, and an interesting display of botanical and artistic talent. |
| Flanagan...... (1 to 7) | The History of New South Wales. By R. Flanagan. London, 1862. 2 vols. 8vo. | Carefully compiled, and forms a very trustworthy and unprejudiced source of information. Has an index. |
| Flinders ...... (1) | Voyage to Terra Australis, 1801-3. London, 1814. 2 vols. 4to. Atlas, fol. | Contains an account of the survey of the East Coast of Australia, its scenery, climate, &c. |

| Mode of Reference. | Full Title, &c. | Remarks. |
|---|---|---|
| Ford ......... (1) | Ford's Sydney Commercial Directory for 1851. Sydney. 12mo. | In addition to the Directory, it contains a list of the public and private Institutions in Sydney. |
| Ford ......... (7) | Australian Almanac and Repository of Useful Knowledge. Published by W. and F. Ford. Sydney, 1850-54. 12mo. | With the exception of an account of the Revenues of New South Wales and a Table of Public Statutes, it does not contain much information respecting the Colony. |
| Forster ...... (4.5) | Land and Squatting Question reconsidered. By William Forster. Sydney, 1855. 8vo. Pamph. pp. 32. | Valuable suggestions for the occupation of Crown Lands. Squatting system, plan of tendering for runs, etc. |
| Fowler......... (4) | Southern Lights and Shadows. By Frank Fowler. London, 1859. 12mo. | A very amusing, but for the most part erroneous and misleading account of Colonial life. |
| Fowles......... (1) | Sydney in 1848, illustrated by copperplate Engravings. From Drawings of Joseph Fowles. Sydney, 1848. 4to. | Gives a general and accurate description of the City of Sydney, its Public Buildings, Institutions, &c. |
| Francis ...... (4.5) | The present and future Government of New South Wales. By Henry Francis. Sydney, 1869. 8vo. Pamph. pp. 48. | Refers to Parliamentary corruption and Reform, Revenue and Expenditure, Railways, Magistracy, Public Buildings, &c. |
| Free Public Library. | Catalogue of the Free Public Library, Sydney, 1876. Sydney, 1878. Roy. 8vo. | The Library contained, at the end of 1876, about 30,000 vols., including upwards of 800 works relating to Australasia. |
| Fulton......... (4.5) | A letter to the Rev. W. B. Ullathorne, C.K.G., in answer to "A few words to the Rev. H. Fulton and his readers." By the Rev. H. Fulton. Sydney, 1833. 8vo. Pamph. pp. 54. | Controversial. See "Ullathorne." |
| Fulton......... (4) | Strictures on a letter lately written by Roger Therry, Esq., in New South Wales, to Edward Blount, Esq., M.P. By the Rev. H. Fulton, A.B., Chaplain of Castlereagh, in New South Wales. Sydney, 1833. 8vo. Pamph. pp. 39. | One of a series of letters discussing the propriety of Protestants assisting towards the erection of St. Mary's (Roman Catholic) Cathedral. |
| Geddes ...... (3) | Colonial Agriculture. A course of four Lectures delivered in the School of Arts, Maitland, during the year 1845. By William Geddes. Sydney, 1855. 8vo. Pamph. pp. 40. | Gives valuable statistical information, and also suggestions as to crops that might be profitably grown in the Colony. |
| Geological ... (3) | Geological Topographical Sketches of the Province of New Ulster. 8vo. Pamph. pp. 28. | Though treating principally of the Geology of New Ulster, a province of New Zealand, several pages are devoted to the geology and to the then recently discovered auriferous deposits of New South Wales. |

| Mode of Reference. | Full Title, &c. | Remarks. |
|---|---|---|
| Gerstæcker ... (1.5) | Narrative of a Journey round the World. By F. Gerstæcker. London, 1853. 3 vols. 8vo. | The third volume contains a description of Sydney in 1851, at the time of the discovery of gold in the Colony. |
| Gordon ...... (3.7) | The Australian Handbook and Almanac, and Shippers and Importers' Directory for 1876. London (Gordon & Gotch). 8vo. | Contains the most recent information with reference to the resources, trade, population, and general statistics of the Colony. |
| Gould ......... (3) | The Birds of Australia. By John Gould, F.R.S. London, 1848. 7 vols. fol. The Mammals of Australia. London, 1863. 3 vols. fol. By John Gould, F.R.S. | One of the most valuable contributions to the Natural History of Australia. |
| Graham ...... (4) | Lawrence Struilby; or observations and experiences during twenty-five years of bush life in Australia. Edited by John Graham. London, 1863. 12mo. | Incidental sketches of bush life, and gives a truthful picture of the habits and character of the Aborigines. |
| Gray ......... (3) | The Lizards of Australia and New Zealand. By J. E. Gray, Ph. D. London, 1867. 4to. | An important contribution to the Natural History of the Colony. |
| Greenwood ... (4.5) | New South Wales Public School League for making Primary Education National, Secular, Compulsory, and Free. Summary of facts and principles. By Jas. Greenwood, M.A. Sydney, 1874. 8vo. Pamph. pp. 16. | Opposed to the present system of Denominational Education. |
| Greville ...... (1 to 7) | Greville's Official Post Office Directory and Gazetteer of New South Wales. 1875 to 1877. Sydney, 1876. 8vo. | Full of information on almost every subject relating to the Colony, to the latest date. |
| Griffiths ...... (3.4.5) | The present state and prospects of the Port Phillip District of New South Wales. By Charles Griffiths. Post 8vo. Dublin, 1845. | Gives an account of that part of the Colony before separation; its population, squatting system, &c. |
| Gurner......... (5) | Chronicle of Port Phillip, now the Colony of Victoria, from 1770 to 1840. By Henry Field Gurner. Melbourne, 1876. 8vo. Pamph. pp. 52. | An apparently very correct compilation. Refers in some measure to the past history of New South Wales. |
| Hannaford ... (3) | Jottings in Australia; or Notes on the Flora and Fauna of Victoria. By S. Hannaford. Melbourne, 1856. 12mo. | A useful little book. Has some reference to the Botany of New South Wales. |
| Hargraves ... (3.5) | Australia and its Gold Fields. By E. H. Hargraves. London, 1855. 12mo. | Relates to the discovery and theories as to the source of gold in Australia. |
| Harvey ...... (3) | Phycologia Australica; or, a History of Australian Seaweeds. By W. H. Harvey, M.D., &c. London, 1858. 5 vols. Roy. 8vo. | Gives ample and interesting information on Australian Marine Botany, with description of the Marine Algæ of New South Wales. |

| Mode of Reference. | Full Title, &c. | Remarks. |
|---|---|---|
| Haygarth ... (4) | Recollections of Bush Life in Australia. By the Rev. H. W. Haygarth. London, 1861. 12mo. | Gives a truthful description of life in the interior of the Colony. |
| Hellicar ...... (3.8) | Coin and Currency ; being an inquiry into the probable effect of legalizing as currency the coinage of the Sydney Mint. By Valentine Hellicar. Melbourne, 1856. 8vo. | Written to oppose the recognition in Victoria of coin issued by the Sydney Mint. |
| Henderson ... (2.4) | Excursions and Adventures in New South Wales. By J. Henderson. London, 1851. 2 vols. 12mo. | A true account of the climate of New South Wales, and of the manners and customs of the colonists, &c., at the time it was written. |
| Henderson ... (3) | Observations on the Colonies of New South Wales, &c. By John Henderson. Calcutta, 1832. 8vo. | Refers principally to the political economy and natural history of the Colony. Written about the year 1830. |
| Hill .......... (4) | What we saw in Australia. By R. and F. Hill. London, 1875. 8vo. | An excellent and truthful description of the Colony, especially with reference to the various Public and Charitable Institutions at the present time. |
| Hodgkinson... (1.3.4.) | Australia, from Port Macquarie to Moreton Bay, with description of the Natives, their manners and customs, etc. By Clement Hodgkinson. London, 1845. 8vo. | A faithful description of the physical aspect of the country — its rivers, mountains, etc. ; and of the aborigines—their wars, festivals, etc. |
| Hodgson ...... (3.4) | Reminiscences of Australia. By C. P. Hodgson. London, 1846. 12mo. | Relates principally to life in the interior of the Colony, productions, &c. |
| Holman ...... (1) | Voyage round the World, including Africa, Asia, Australasia, &c. By Jas. Holman. London, 1834. 4 vols. 8vo. | In the fourth volume there is a short description of New South Wales. |
| Holt.......... (4.5) | Two Speeches on the subject of Education in New South Wales. Delivered in the Legislative Assembly, Sydney, by the Hon. Thos. Holt, Esq., M.P. Sydney, 1857. Pamph. pp. 39. | An exposition of the principles of State Education, showing the connection between vice and ignorance. An exposé of both the Denominational and National systems as at present conducted, and offers suggestions for the alteration of the educational system of the Colony. |
| Hood ........ (2 to 5) | Australia and the East; being a Journal narrative of a voyage to N.S.W. in an emigrant ship, with a residence of some months in Sydney and the bush, etc. By John Hood. London, 1843. 8vo. | Gives a sketch of the history and productions of the Colony, and of life in the bush, with some account of the aborigines, climate, &c. |
| Hooker ...... (3) | On the Flora of Australia — its origin, affinities, and distribution. B. J. D. Hooker, M.D. London, 1859. 4to. | Contains valuable botanical information in connection with the Colony. |

| Mode of Reference. | Full Title, &c. | Remarks. |
|---|---|---|
| Hornby ...... (4) | The Cruise round the World of the Flying Squadron, 1869-70, under the command of Rear-Admiral G. T. Phipps Hornby. (By Lieut. Bruce.) London, 1871. 8vo. | An inaccurate and absurd account of the state of society in Sydney. |
| Horne ......... (4) | Australian Facts and Prospects. By R. H. Horne. London, 1859. 12mo. | The small portion which refers to New South Wales gives a fairly correct view of Colonial society, &c. |
| Horticultural Magazine (3) | Horticultural Magazine and Gardener's Calendar of New South Wales. Sydney, 1865. 8vo. | Full of information on all subjects connected with Colonial gardening. |
| Houlding ... (4) | Rural and City Life; or the Fortunes of the Stubble Family. By Old Boomerang (J. R. Houlding). London, 1870. 8vo. | A most amusing story of Australian life, full of humour, and containing some picturesque descriptions of Australian scenery. |
| Houlding ... (4) | Australian Capers; or, Christopher Cockle's Colonial Experience. By Old Boomerang (J. R. Houlding). London, 1867. 8vo. | A fictitious but very humourous account of the adventures of an immigrant in Australia. Throws a good deal of light upon the manners and peculiarities of the Colonists. |
| Houlding...... (4) | Australian Tales and Sketches from Real Life. By Old Boomerang (J. R. Houlding). London, 1868. 8vo. | Lively and clever sketches, abounding with incident peculiar to Australia. |
| Hovell ...... (4.5) | An Answer to the Preface to the second edition of Mr. Hamilton Hume's "A Brief Statement of Facts." By W. H. Hovell. Sydney (ca.) 1855. Pamph. 8vo. pp. 10. | This was written in refutation of certain charges brought against him by Hume (q. v.) in connection with the overland journey to Port Phillip. |
| Hovell and Hume. (1.5) | Journey of Discovery to Port Phillip in 1824-25. By W. H. Hovell and H. Hume. Edited by W. Bland. Sydney, 1837. 8vo. | An early, interesting, and trustworthy description of the interior of New South Wales. |
| Howard ...... (3.4) | Biographical Sketch of the late Allan Cunningham, Esq., F.L.S., M.R.G.S., &c. By Robert Howard, F.L.S. London, 1842. 8vo. | An account of the Botany of New South Wales, as described by the indefatigable and ill-fated botanist, Allan Cunningham. |
| Howe ......... (3 to 7) | New South Wales Pocket Almanack. Compiled and printed by George Howe. Sydney, 1808-26. 12mo. | Contains a great deal of information on almost all subjects of interest connected with the Colony. |
| Howe ......... (3 to 7) | Australian Almanack. Edited, printed, and compiled by Robert Howe. Sydney, 1827-32. 12mo. | Same as the foregoing. |
| Howitt......... (1.5) | Australia: Historical, Descriptive, and Statistic. By R. Howitt. London, 1845. 12mo. | Gives a correct description of Australia generally, but little reference is made to New South Wales. |
| Howitt ....... (1.5) | The History of Discovery in Australia, Tasmania, and New Zealand, from the earliest date to the present day. By William Howitt. London, 1865. 2 vols. 8vo. | Refers, with the exception of an excellent account of the discoveries of the Portugese and Dutch, almost exclusively to expeditions into the interior of the Colony. |

| Mode of Reference. | Full Title, &c. | Remarks. |
|---|---|---|
| Hughes ...... (2.3.4) | The Australian Colonies, their origin and present condition. By W. Hughes. London, 1852. 12mo. | A short but correct account of the Colony, with remarks on the climate, &c. |
| Hume ......... (1.4.5) | A Brief Statement of Facts in connection with an overland expedition from Lake George to Port Phillip, in 1824. By Hamilton Hume. Third edition. Yass, 1874. 8vo. | The object of this statement was to show that the expedition under Hovell and Hume (q. v.) was conducted by Hume, and that to his exertions its success was chiefly owing. |
| Hunter ...... (1.2.5) | Historical Journal of the Transactions at Port Jackson and Norfolk Island. By John Hunter, R.N. Lond., 1793. 4to. | A diary of events, from the sailing of the first expedition under Captain Phillip to the beginning of the year 1792. Written by a former Governor of the Colony. |
| Illustrated Sydney News. (3.5) | Illustrated Sydney News Almanac (Saxby) for 1865. Published by Clarson, Shallard & Co. Sydney. 8vo. | Contains, besides other information, an apparently correct statistical view of the progress of New South Wales, from 1859 to 1863. |
| Immigration (4.5) | Debate in the Legislative Council of New South Wales, and other documents, on the subject of Immigration to the Colony. Published under the direction of the Australian Immigration Association. Sydney, 1840. 8vo. Pamph. pp. 51. | "In short, any sacrifice must be made rather than not have Emigrants: Emigrants the Colony must have, by some means or other." Mr. R. Jones' speech.<br><br>See also Emigration. |
| Immigration (4.5) | Fund for promoting Female Emigration. First Report of the Committee. London, 1851. 8vo. Pamph. pp. 87. | Shows the readiness with which all respectable females were provided with suitable employment at good wages on their arrival at Sydney. |
| Immigration (4.5) | Expenditure of the Land Fund of New South Wales in the Colony, and principally on Public Works, as a means of promoting and supporting Immigration. Sydney, 1842. 8vo. Pamph. pp. 24. | Advocates the prosecution of Public Works as a means of encouraging Immigration by creating a demand for labour. |
| Immigration (4.5) | A few copies of letters, and some remarks upon sundry documents on the subject of Female Emigration. By the Superintendent of the "Layton," emigrant ship. Sydney, 1836. Pamph. pp. 32. | Exposes the careless manner in which the system was worked in 1836, and its fearful effect on public morals. |
| Immigration (4,5) | Thoughts on Emigration. By an Old Colonist. Bathurst, 1856. Pamph. pp. 12. | In favour of a free, self-supporting system of Immigration. |
| Immigration . (4.5) | Bounty Immigration. A letter to the Members of the Legislative Council. By "One who has handled the Spade." Melbourne, 1855. 8vo. Pamph. pp. 71. | Opposed to the bounty system and assisted Immigration, on the ground that the labouring classes in the Colony would suffer by the introduction of others of the same class. |

| Mode of Reference. | Full Title, &c. | Remarks. |
|---|---|---|
| Immigration . (3.4.5) | The Emigrant's Guide to New South Wales, Van Diemen's Land, Lower Canada, Upper Canada, and New Brunswick, containing an enumeration of the advantages which each Colony offers; with the Regulations adopted by His Majesty's Government to facilitate Male and Female Emigration; the price of passage, etc., etc. By the Emigration Commissioners. London, 1832. 8vo. Pamph. pp. 34. | Gives market prices at Sydney in 1832, and other statistical and general information of use to intending Emigrants. |
| Immigration . (3.4.5) | An impartial examination of all the Authors on Australia, Official Documents, and the Reports of private individuals, as evidences of the advantages of Emigration, etc., etc. By an Intending Emigrant. London, 1838. 12mo. pp. 92. | A very useful compilation, affording a large amount of reliable information on a variety of subjects. |
| James ......... (1.3.4.) | Six months in South Australia, with some account of Port Philip and Portland Bay, in Australia Felix; with advice to Emigrants, &c., &c. By T. Horton James. London, 1838. 12mo. | In addition to a short description of Sydney the book contains an account of a "ride of six hundred miles from Sydney to Melbourne, through the district of Illawarra." |
| Jameson ...... (2.3.4.) | New Zealand, South Australia, and New South Wales; a record of recent travels in these Colonies. By R. G. Jameson. London, 1842. 12mo. | Contains useful information on agriculture, trade, climate, productions, and Colonial society. |
| Jenkins ........ (4.5) | Universal Education. A lecture by R. L. Jenkins, Esq., M.L.A., on 21st Nov., 1859. Together with Petitions presented to Parliament. Sydney, 1859. Pamph. pp. 57. | In favour of free education, the funds to be raised by tea and sugar duties. |
| Jobson......... (1.4.) | Australia; with notes by the way, on Egypt, Ceylon, Bombay, and the Holy Land. By F. J. Jobson, D.D. London, 1862. 8vo. | Gives a short description of Sydney and Suburbs, with remarks on the state of Religion in the Colony. |
| Johnson ....... (1) | Questions on Australian and General Geography. By Miss Johnson. Sydney, 1870. 16mo. | A useful little book, in the form of questions and answers. |
| Johnston...... (3) | The Art of Farming, adapted to the Colonies. By William Johnston. Sydney, 1873. 8vo. Pamph. pp. 53. | Relates to the properties of the soil, the effects of the climate on the vegetable productions, breeding and rearing of stock, &c. |
| Judges......... (4.5.) | The Judges' Salaries Act. The measure explained and vindicated, in a letter to E. C. Weekes, Esq., M.L.A. By Fair Play. Sydney, 1857. Pamph. pp. 9. | Shows the increased cost of the necessaries of life in the Colonies, and the extension of the responsibilities and labours of the Judges, as a reason for more liberal salaries. |
| Jukes .......... (1.3.) | A Sketch of the Physical Structure of Australia. By J. Beete Jukes, M.A. London, 1850. 8vo. | A short but valuable and accurate account of the geological structure of the country. |

| Mode of Reference. | Full Title, &c. | Remarks. |
|---|---|---|
| Jukes........ (1.3.) | Lectures on Gold, for the instruction of Emigrants about to proceed to Australia. By J. B. Jukes and others. London, 1852. 8vo. | An interesting paper on the Geology of Australia. |
| Kelly.......... (4) | Lord Roger in his War Paint. By John E. Kelly. Sydney, 1876. 12mo. Pamph. pp. 111. | Written by the Editor of the "Stockwhip," and refers to Archbishop Vaughan's Advent Conference Pamphlets (q. v.) |
| Kendall....... (3.4) | Leaves from Australian Forests. By H. Kendall. Melbourne, 1869. 12mo. Poems and Songs. By H. Kendall. Sydney, 1862. 12mo. | "Consists almost entirely of descriptive poems. . . . The author paints the scenery of his native land with the hand of a master."—Barton's Literature in N.S.W. |
| Kennedy...... (1.4.5) | Enquiry taken at Sydney, before J. L. Innes, Esq., and H. H. Browne, Esq., relative to the death of E. B. C. Kennedy and others, who left Sydney on an exploring expedition in Tropical Australia on the 29th day of April, 1848. (MS.) | The sad fate of Kennedy, who was speared by the blacks, and the fidelity of his black boy, Jacky Jacky, give special interest to this expedition. Mr. W. Carron, one of the survivors of the Expedition, was for many years connected with the Botanical Gardens, Sydney. |
| Kennedy...... (1 to 5) | Extracts from the Journal of an Exploring Expedition into Central Australia, to determine the course of the River Barcoo (Victoria) 1847-8. By E. B. Kennedy, Esq. With Notes by the Rev. W. B. Clarke, M.A. London. 8vo. Pamph. pp. 54. | A thoroughly scientific and practical report of the country traversed. The party was subjected to great privations at times for want of water. Kennedy generally reports favourably of the conduct of the blacks met with. Meteorological Journal, with Notes by Rev. W. B. Clarke. |
| Kentish ...... (4.5) | Thoughts on the proposed Address and Petition of the Colonists of New South Wales to the King. By N. L. Kentish, Esq. Sydney, 1831. 8vo. Pamph. pp. 41. | Refers to the Church and Corporation Lands, the promotion of Emigration, to the discontinuance of transportation, and to the Government Order discontinuing the disposal of unlocated land by grant, and requiring immediate payment of all arrears of "quit rent." |
| Kentish ...... (4.5) | Political Economy of N.S.W., developed in a series of letters addressed to the Colonists themselves, on the present state and future prospects of this interesting, important, and peculiar Colony. Also, the Memorial of the Colonists on several important subjects to the Queen, Lords and Commons, by N. L. Kentish. Sydney, 1838. 8vo. Pamph. pp. 52. | Refers to the withdrawal of convict labour, and suggests an extensive and permanent tide of immigration from the United Kingdom. The memorial appended is a petition for the continuance of transportation and assignment system. |
| King ......... (2) | Abstract from a Meteorological Journal kept at Port Stephens, New South Wales, during the years 1843 to 1847, by Captain Phillip, P. King, R.N., F.R.S. Tasmania. 8vo. pp. 4. | Contains a table giving the monthly mean temperature and evaporation for five years. |
| King ......... (3) | Australia may be an extensive wine-growing country. By James King. Edinburgh, 1857. 8vo. Pamph. pp. 10, and Mr. King's Wine Report, 1851. pp. 8. | Contains useful and trustworthy information as to the progress made in the production of wine in the Colony. |

| Mode of Reference. | Full Title, &c. | Remarks. |
|---|---|---|
| Kingston ...... (2) | Diagrams showing the average monthly rainfall in Adelaide, Melbourne, and Sydney, 1839–74, as registered by Sir C. S. Kingston. Adelaide, 1874, fol. | These diagrams show the average monthly and the maximum and minimum rainfall in each month, compiled from official records. That part relating to Sydney dates from 1840 to 1874. |
| Knaggs ...... (3) | The Newcastle Business Directory, and Hunter River District Almanac, published by R. C. Knaggs and Co. Newcastle, 1870–76. 8vo. Newcastle Nautical Almanac, published by R. C. Knaggs and Co. Newcastle, 1874–75. 8vo. | Contain statistics of the Port of Newcastle, and other information. |
| Krefft ......... (3) | The Snakes of Australia; an illustrated and descriptive Catalogue of all the known species. By Gerard Krefft, F.L.S., &c. Sydney, 1869. 4to. | A valuable addition to the natural history of New South Wales. |
| Krefft ......... (3) | Catalogue of Mammalia in the collection of the Australian Museum. By Gerard Krefft. Sydney, 1864. 12mo. | Contains a list of a large number of mounted examples of Australian Mammals. |
| Labillardière (3) | Novæ Hollandiæ Plantarum Specimen Auctore J. J. de Labillardière. Paris, 1804. 2 vols. 4to. | An important work on the Botany of Australia. |
| Lands ......... (5) | Report from the Select Committee on the disposal of Lands in the British Colonies. London, August 1st, 1836. Folio. | W. W. Whitmore, E. G. Wakefield, and Colonel Torrens, examined in reference to the proper mode of disposal of land in Australia. |
| Lands ......... (4.5) | Alienation of Crown Lands. The Crown Lands Acts, with the Regulations and Forms thereunder; also the Commons Regulation Act. Sydney, 1873. 8vo. | This volume contains all the Regulations at present in force relative to the occupation of the Land. A most comprehensive fund of information. |
| Lands ......... (4.5) | Report of the Debate on the Alienation of Crown Lands in New South Wales, in the House of Commons, on Thursday, 7th June, 1832. London, 1832. 8vo. Pamph. pp. 16. | Refers to a Government Order, issued in Sydney in 1831, by which the Regulations then in force respecting grants of lands in New South Wales were withdrawn, and others promulgated. |
| Lands ......... (4.5) | The Land Question familiarly and practically considered, by a Practical Man. Sydney, 1856. 8vo. Pamph. pp. 27. | Pre-emptive right to be allowed to present holders of runs. Runs in proximity to towns stopping settlement, to be resumed. Describes the quality of the land on the different rivers. Objects to the auction system of selling land. |
| Lang ......... (4.5) | Botany Bay. By John Lang, Esq. London, 1859. 12mo. | A most amusing little book. The various legends of the Colony, mostly relating to remarkable convicts, are founded upon truth, though treated in the form of fiction. |
| Lang ......... (4.5) | Freedom and Independence for the Golden Lands of Australia. By the Rev. J. D. Dr. Lang, D.D. London, 1852. 12mo. | Relates to the social and political state of the Colony. |

| Mode of Reference. | Full Title, &c. | Remarks. |
|---|---|---|
| Lang .........<br>(1 to 7) | An Historical and Statistical Account of New South Wales. By J. D. Lang, D.D., &c. Fourth edition. London, 1875. 2 vols. 8vo. | An ample and minute account of New South Wales, containing most interesting information, from the discovery of Australia to the year 1874. Full of correct statistical extracts. A review of the third edition of this work is given in Barton's "Literature in New South Wales," p. 124. |
| Lang .........<br>(3.4) | Poems, Sacred and Secular. By J. D. Lang, D.D., &c. Sydney, 1873. 12mo. | Contains translations of two or three aboriginal songs. In some of the poems, Australian scenery and events are pleasingly portrayed. |
| Lang .........<br>(5) | A letter to the Right Hon. Lord Stanley, occasioned by certain observations in the speech of His Excellency Sir G. Gipps. By J. D. Lang, D.D., &c. Sydney, 1845. 8vo. Pamph. pp. 21. | Refers to various Addresses of the Legislative Council to Her Majesty, praying for alterations in the Constitution. The Governor, in his speech, appears to have imputed to the Council disloyal motives. |
| Lang .........<br>(4.5) | The Question of Questions; or, is this Colony to be transformed into a Province of the Popedom? A letter by J. D. Lang, D.D. Sydney, 1841. 8vo. Pamph. pp. 61. | The object of this letter was to expose certain practices on the part of the London agents; particularly in sending out to the Colony too large a proportion of Roman Catholic immigrants, under the private bounty system. |
| Lang .........<br>(4.5) | Three Lectures on the impolicy and injustice of religious establishments in the Australian Colonies. By J. D. Lang, D.D. Sydney, 1856. 8vo. Pamph. pp. 76. | Directed against the system of State support to religion in New South Wales. |
| Lang .........<br>(5) | The Coming Event! or Freedom and Independence for the seven united Provinces of Australia. By J. D. Lang, D.D., &c. Sydney, 1870. 8vo. | The object of this work is to advise "the speedy and entire political separation of the united Colonies of Australia from the Mother Country, and their erection into a sovereign and independent State." |
| Lang .........<br>(1.3) | Cooksland, in North-eastern Australia. By J. D. Lang, D.D., &c. London, 1847. 12mo. | Gives a good deal of accurate information on the geographical features and the natural and artificial productions of the north-eastern portion of the Colony. |
| Lan .........<br>(4.5) | Transportation and Colonization; or the causes of the comparative failure of the transportation system. By J. D. Lang, D.D., &c. London, 1837. 12mo. | Illustrative of the failure of the transportation system, and points out the extent to which free emigration to the Colony is practicable under the existing land-selling system. |
| Lang .........<br>(4.5) | Free Church Morality in three of its developments in New South Wales. By J. D. Lang, D.D., &c. Sydney, 1876. 8vo. Pamph. pp. 45. | Refers to certain occurrences in connection with the Presbyterian Church in New South Wales; and gives a short history of the founding of St. Andrew's College. |
| Lang .........<br>(5) | Eine deutsche Colonie in stillen Ocean. Von J. D. Lang, Dr. Theol., etc., aus dem englischen übersetzen. Leipzig, 1848. 8vo. pp. 45. | "Another instance of Dr. Lang's indefatigable efforts to promote emigration to this part of the World." *Barton's Literature in N.S.W.* |

| Mode of Reference. | Full Title, &c. | Remarks. |
|---|---|---|
| Lang ......... (4.5) | The Convict's Bank; or a plain statement of the case of alleged embezzlement on the part of Messrs. G. D. Lang and F. L. Drake, of the Branch Bank of New South Wales, at Ballaarat. By J. D. Lang, D.D., &c. Sydney, 1855. 8vo. Pamph. pp. 58. | Refers to a trial which took place in Victoria. It has also reference to New South Wales, and throws some light on Colonial social life, and on the administration of justice in the Colonies twenty years ago. |
| Lang ......... (4.5) | Emigration; considered chiefly in reference to the practicability and expediency of importing and settling throughout the territory of New South Wales a numerous, industrious, and virtuous agricultural population. A lecture; by J. D. Lang, D.D. Sydney, 1833. 8vo. Pamph. pp. 18. | Recommends that the proceeds of all sales of Crown Land be devoted to the encouragement of emigration, and to promote the formation of small agricultural communities throughout the Colony. |
| Lang ......... (4.5) | Narrative of the settlement of the Scots' Church, Sydney. By J. D. Lang, D.D. Sydney, 1828. 8vo. Pamph. pp. 108. | A most interesting account of the origin and progress of the Presbyterian Church in New South Wales. |
| Lang ......... (4.5) | Account of the steps taken in England with a view to the establishment of an Academical Institution or College in New South Wales. By the Rev. J. D. Lang, D.D., &c. Sydney, 1831. 8vo. Pamph. pp. 27. | Refers to an attempt at that date to found a College in Sydney, for the education of youth on the principle of the Schools and Colleges of Scotland. |
| Lang ......... (5) | A Sermon preached on Sunday, June 15th, 1823, to the congregation of Scots' Presbyterians. Sydney, 1823. 8vo. Pamph. pp. 18. | Preached in aid of funds for the erection of a Scots' Church in Sydney. |
| Lang ......... (1.5) | Phillipsland; or the country designated Port Phillip. By J. D. Lang, D.D., &c. London, 1847. 12mo. | Contains a large amount of information, besides an excellent description of the overland route from Sydney to Melbourne. |
| Lang ......... (5) | The Fatal Mistake, or how New South Wales has lost caste in the world through misgovernment in the matter of immigration. By John Dunmore Lang, D.D., &c. Sydney, 1875. 8vo. Pamph. pp. 33. | The object of this pamphlet is to show the impolicy of diverting the revenue derived from land, originally appropriated exclusively to promote immigration, to other purposes. |
| Lavers ......... (3) | Testimonials as to the efficacy of Mr. J. V. Lavers's patented process for preserving in a fresh condition the flesh of animals recently killed. Sydney, 1870. 8vo. Pamph. pp. 18. | Refers to a method for preserving fresh killed Australian meat, partly with the view of supplying the markets of Great Britain and the Continent of Europe. |
| Ledger ......... (3.5) | The Alpaca; its introduction into Australia, and the probabilities of acclimatization there. By George Ledger. Melbourne, 1861. 8vo. Pamph. pp. 35. | Gives a correct history of the introduction of the Alpaca into the Colony, and shows the adaptability of the climate and pasturage of New South Wales to their successful and profitable maintenance. |

| Mode of Reference. | Full Title, &c. | Remarks. |
|---|---|---|
| Leigh .........<br>(1.4) | The Handbook of Sydney and Suburbs. Published by S. T. Leigh & Co. Sydney, 1869. 8vo. | A condensed, but on the whole correct, description of the public buildings and institutions of Sydney, their administration, &c. |
| Lhotsky ......<br>(1.3.4) | Journey from Sydney to the Australian Alps, undertaken in the months of January, February, and March, 1834 ; being an account of the geographical and natural relations of the country traversed, and the Aborigines ; together with some general information of the Colony of New South Wales. By Dr. John Lhotsky. Sydney, 1835. 8vo. | Lhotsky claims the discovery of hot and mineral springs. The book contains other matters of interest. |
| Lindt .........<br>(4) | Australian Aborigines ; photographed by J. W. Lindt. Twelve photographs in portfolio. 4to. Sydney, 1874. | Portraits of Aborigines of the Clarence River District of New South Wales. |
| Linnean Society.<br>(3) | The proceedings of the Linnean Society of New South Wales. Vol. 1. 8 vo. Sydney, 1877. | "Instituted for the cultivation and study of the Science of Natural History in all its branches." |
| Low.............<br>(5) | The City of Sydney Directory for 1844-5 and 1847—Compiled by Francis Low. Sydney. 8vo. | Contains a good deal of useful information, and gives a chronological table of remarkable events. |
| Lowe .........<br>(5) | The impending Crisis ; an Address to the Colonists of New South Wales on the proposed Land Orders. By Robert Lowe, Esq., M.L.C. Sydney, 1847. 8vo. Pamph. pp. 8. | Objects to a proposal to divide the Colony into three districts, viz., settled, intermediate, and unsettled ; and to the regulations for selling and leasing the land in the different districts. |
| Lowe .........<br>(4.5) | Speech of Robert Lowe, Esq., Member of the Legislative Council of New South Wales, for the City of Sydney, on Tuesday, 7th August, 1849. Sydney, 1849. 8vo. Pamph. pp. 30. | In reference to a so-called Consistorial Court in the case of the Rev. Mr. Russell. Mr. Lowe objects to the Bishop's course of procedure. |
| Lowe .........<br>(5) | Speech on the Australian Colonies' Bill. By Robert Lowe, Esq., late Member for Sydney. June 1st, 1850. 8vo. Pamph. pp. 32. | Suggests reduction of the qualification for franchise ; a Constitution of two Chambers ; not in favour of a Federal Government for Australia. |
| Lutwyche ...<br>(5) | Electoral Reform : Report of a speech delivered in the Legislative Council by the Hon. Alfred J. P. Lutwyche. Sydney, 1858. 8vo. Pamph. pp. 35. | Favourable to reform, but opposed to vote by ballot. |
| Lycett .........| Views in Australia ; or, New South Wales and Van Diemen's Land ; delineated in 50 views, with descriptive letter-press. Dedicated by permission to Earl Bathurst, &c. 1 vol. Oblong 4to. London, 1824. Another edition with colored plates. 1827. | Not in the Free Public Library, Sydney ; no reference to be found. |

C

| Mode of Reference. | Full Title, &c. | Remarks. |
|---|---|---|
| M'Arthur ... (1.3.6) | New South Wales; its present state and future prospects. By James M'Arthur. London, 1837. 8vo. | Treats of the general resources of the Colony, administration of justice, &c. |
| M'Arthur ... (5) | Critical examination of Mr. James M'Arthur's work on New South Wales. Sydney, 1838. | Not in the Free Public Library, Sydney. |
| M'Arthur ... (5) | Review of the examination of Mr. James M'Arthur's work "New South Wales, its present state, and future prospects"; from the Australian newspapers. Sydney, 1839. | Condemns Mr. M'Arthur's work (q. v.) as full of false assertions and opinions, and upholds the author of the "Examination" as likely "to counteract whatever unjust impressions Mr. M'Arthur's book may have produced." |
| Macarthur ... (4.5) | Colonial policy of 1840 and 1841, as illustrated by the Governor's despatches, and proceedings of the Legislative Council of New South Wales, By Major Macarthur. London, 1841. 8vo. Pamph. pp. 79. | Has reference to the Lands' Regulations, immigration, and the erection of Victoria into a separate Colony. |
| M'Culloch ... (1 to 7) | Dictionary, Geographical, Statistical, and Historical, of the various countries, places, and principal natural objects in the world. By J. R. M'Culloch, revised by Frederick Martin. London, 1866. 4 vols. Roy. 8vo. | The articles on Australasia and Australia are lengthy, and show considerable research in their preparation; most of the principal voyagers and explorers having been consulted. The statistics of the Colony are given to 1864; and the soil, climate, natural history, ethnology, and geology, as well as the commerce of the Colonies, are all brought under notice. |
| M'Farland ... (1.3) | Illawarra and Manaro Districts of New South Wales. By Alfred M'Farland. Sydney, 1872. 12mo. | A most trustworthy account of the productions, trade, &c., of that part of New South Wales. |
| Mackay ...... (3) | The Sugar-cane in Australia. Edited by Angus Mackay. Brisbane, 1870. 8vo. | Contains remarks on the New South Wales Sugar Crop, &c. |
| Mackay ...... (3.5) | The great Gold Field. A pedestrian tour through the first discovered Gold Field of New South Wales, in the months of October and November, 1852. By Angus Mackay. Sydney, 1853. 8vo. Pamph. pp. 68. | Very interesting, as giving the evidence of an eye-witness of the large yields of gold obtained at the different Gold Fields when first opened. |
| Mackenzie ... (1.2.3.4) | Ten Years in Australia. By the Rev. D. Mackenzie. London, 1852. 12mo. | Gives a short description of "bush life," and of the country generally to about 1852. |
| Macleay ...... (5) | Correspondence with His Excellency Sir Richard Bourke, K.C.B., and other documents relative to the removal of A. Macleay, Esq., from the office of Colonial Secretary of New South Wales. | Mr. Macleay having voted in opposition to the Governor, the latter wrote to England stating that Mr. Macleay had expressed his intention of resigning. A successor to the office was accordingly sent out, and arrived in the Colony before Mr. Macleay was aware of the Governor's altered feeling towards him. |

| Mode of Reference. | Full Title, &c. | Remarks. |
|---|---|---|
| Maclehose ... (1.3.4.5) | Picture of Sydney, and Stranger's Guide in New South Wales for 1838. Edited by J. Maclehose. Sydney, 1838. 12mo. | A truthful description of Sydney about the year 1838, and contains a great deal of interesting historical and statistical information. |
| Macpherson .. (4) | My experience in Australia. By a Lady (Mrs. Macpherson). London, 1860. 12mo. | Contains much useful information relative to every-day life in the Colony. |
| Macqueen ... (3.4.5) | Australia as she is and as she may be. By T. Potter Macqueen, Esq. London, 1840. 8vo. Pamph. pp. 60. | Treats of convicts and free immigrants. Contrasts the condition of both with that of agricultural labourers in England. Suggests cultivation of various important products, and refers to the pastoral resources of the Colony. |
| Magistrates... (4.5) | Return to an Address of the Honorable the House of Commons, dated 17th April, 1826, for copies of papers relating to the conduct of Magistrates in New South Wales, in directing the infliction of punishments upon prisoners in that Colony. Sydney, 1855. 8vo. Pamph. pp. 22. | The flogging system. The Grand Jury found that the acts of Magisterial authority were beyond the law, opposed to the principles of reformation and the interests and welfare of society. |
| Majoribanks.. (3.4.5) | Travels in New South Wales. By Alex. Majoribanks. London, 1847. 12mo. | Treats chiefly of the Colony during the time it was a penal settlement, but contains also information relative to the suburbs of Sydney and general society. |
| Mann ......... (3.4) | Six years residence in the Australian Provinces. By W. Mann. London, 1839. 12mo. | That part referring to New South Wales contains information on the trade, population, resources, &c., of the Colony. |
| Manning ...... (1.5) | Review on the Report of William Clark, Esq., Hydraulic Engineer, on the question of water supply for Sydney. By James Manning, Esq. Sydney, 1877. 8vo. Pamph. pp. 75. | Opposed to the course recommended by Mr. Clark (q.v.) for supplying Sydney with water. |
| Mansfield ... (2.3.4) | Analytical View of the Census of New South Wales, for the years 1841 and 1846, with Tables showing the progress of the population during the last twenty-five years, and an Appendix. By Ralph Mansfield. Sydney, 1847. 8vo. Pamph. pp. 144. | Most valuable statistical information, systematically arranged, in reference to the population of the Colony, its Revenue from 1836 to 1845; land under cultivation and live stock; with an Appendix (Meteorology by G.E.P.) |
| Markham ... (5) | Commodore J. G. Goodenough. A brief Memoir by Clements R. Markham, C. B. Portsmouth and London, 1876. 12mo. | A short review of the life of a Naval Commander for several years stationed in the Australian waters. |
| Marriage Act (4.5) | The decision of the Three Judges of the Supreme Court of N.S.W. on the applicability of the Marriage Act of England to this Colony. Sydney, 1836. 8vo. Pamph. pp. 39. | Decided that the English Marriage Act did not extend to the Colonies. |

| Mode of Reference. | Full Title, &c. | Remarks. |
|---|---|---|
| Marsden ...... (4.5) | Memoirs of the life and labours of the Rev. Samuel Marsden. Edited by the Rev. J. B. Marsden. London, 1858. 12mo. | Full of interesting historical and social information relating to the Colony. |
| Marshall ...... (4.5) | Letter to Lord John Russell on Australian Emigration. By W. Marshall. London, 1841. 8vo. Pamph. pp. 26. | In favour of a bounty system. Mr. Marshall claims to have sent over 20,000 emigrants in 80 ships. |
| Martin......... (3.4.5) | Australia, comprising New South Wales, Victoria or Port Phillip, South Australia, and Western Australia. By R. M. Martin. London. 1853. 4to. | An historical and statistical account of the Colony. Some of the statements are incorrect and contradictory. |
| Martin......... (2 to 6) | History of the British Colonies. By R. M. Martin. London, 1835. 5 vols., 8vo. | A small portion of the fourth volume contains useful information on the History, Geology, Climate, Productions, Government, &c., of New South Wales. |
| Martin......... (5) | Statistics of the Colonies of the British Empire, etc.; comprising area, agriculture, commerce, manufactures, shipping, etc., etc., from Records of the Colonial Office. By Robert Montgomery Martin. With Appendix. London, 1839. 8vo. | Gives a brief history of the progress of the Colony through its early struggles down to 1836. |
| Martin......... (1 to 6) | History of Austral-Asia : comprising New South Wales, Van Diemen's Land, Swan River, South Australia, etc. By R. M. Martin, F.S.S. London, 1836. 12mo. | About 200 pp. of this volume are occupied by an interesting account of New South Wales. It touches on almost every topic relating to the Colony. |
| Martineau ... (1.3.4) | Letters from Australia. By John Martineau. 8vo. London, 1869. | Has some references to political and social topics, and gives a description of Sydney and its neighbourhood. |
| Mason and Moore ...... (1.5) | Captain Cook and Botany Bay; with numerous Illustrations from original sketches by Walter Mason. Edited by J. Sheridan Moore. Sydney, 1863. Pamph., pp. 16. | A brief account of the discovery of the Colony. |
| Melville ...... (4.5) | Australasia and Prison Discipline. (By James Melville.) London, 1851. 8vo. | Gives a short account of the Colony as it was in 1847. |
| Meredith...... (4.5) | Notes and Sketches of New South Wales. By Mrs. Charles Meredith. London, 1849. 12mo. | A short but interesting account of Sydney and other parts of the Colony from 1839 to 1844. |
| Mereweather (1.4) | Diary of a Working Clergyman in Australia and Tasmania, kept during the years 1850-53. By the Rev. John Davies Mereweather, B.A. London, 1859. 12mo. | Gives an apparently correct description of Sydney, about the year 1852. |

| Mode of Reference. | Full Title, &c. | Remarks. |
|---|---|---|
| Merewether (4.5) | University of Sydney: Central secular teachings in the schools of the University, combined with distinctive religious teaching and tutorial instruction and discipline in Colleges within the University. Speech by the Hon. F. L. S. Merewether. Sydney, 1858. 8vo., pamph., pp. 27. | A speech delivered in the Legislative Council on the second reading of the Colleges Act Amendment Bill. |
| Mills (1.5.6) | Colonial Constitutions. By Arthur Mills, Esq. London, 1856. 8vo. | This work, among other information, gives a brief outline of the history and political condition of New South Wales. It also contains a list of the Orders of Council, Parliamentary Papers, and Acts relating to the Colony from 1786 to 1855. |
| Milner (4.5) | The Cruise of H.M.S. "Galatea," Captain H.R.H. the Duke of Edinburgh, K.G., in 1867 and 1868. By Rev. J. Milner and O. W. Brierley. London, 1869. 8vo. | That part which refers to N. S. Wales gives an account of O'Farrell's attempt on the Duke's life. |
| Mitchel (4.5) | Jail Journal; or, Five Years in British Prisons. By John Mitchel. New York, 1854. 12mo. | Gives a description of Tasmania, and slightly alludes to New South Wales. |
| Mitchell (1.5) | Exploring Expedition under Sir Thomas Mitchell. Sydney (ca.) 1847. 12mo., pp. 18. | Two despatches to his Excellency the Governor, dated September 9th and November 9th, 1846, from the Rivers Salvator and Balonne. Gives an excellent description of the country near the junction of the Macquarie with the Darling. |
| Mitchell (1 to 5) | Journal of an Expedition into the interior of tropical Australia in search of a route from Sydney to the Gulf of Carpentaria. By Lieut.-Colonel Sir T. L. Mitchell. London, 1848. 8vo. Three Expeditions into the Interior of Eastern Australia, with descriptions of the recently explored region of Australia Felix, and of the present Colony of New South Wales. By Lieut.-Colonel Sir T. L. Mitchell. London, 1838. 2 vols., 8vo. | These Expeditions must be classed among the most memorable in the annals of exploration. The Journals are additionally valuable from the immense amount of scientific information they contain. |
| Mitchell (1.3) | The Australian Geography. By Sir T. L. Mitchell. Sydney, 1851. 12mo. | Gives a brief but accurate description of Australia, arranged by Question and Answer. |
| Mitchell (1.4.5) | Report upon the progress made in Roads, and in the construction of Public Works in New South Wales, from the year 1827 to June, 1855. By Colonel Sir T. L. Mitchell, Surveyor General. Sydney, 1856. Fol. | The value of this work, including the many important illustrations, may be highly estimated, forming as it does a complete and authentic history of the origin and progress of Roads and other Public Works of the Colony. |

| Mode of Reference. | Full Title, &c. | Remarks. |
|---|---|---|
| Monteagle ... (5) | Australia. The substance of three Speeches made in the House of Lords on the Australian Government Bill. By the Lord Monteagle, F.R.S. London, 1850. 8vo. Pamph., pp. 35. | "That there shall be within each of the said Colonies of New South Wales and Victoria a Legislative Council and a Representative Assembly." |
| Moore ......... (3) | On the Woods of New South Wales. By Chas. Moore, Esq., F.L.S., &c. Sydney, 1871. 8vo. Pamph. pp. 44. | An excellent and trustworthy account of the woods and timber trees of New South Wales. |
| Moore ......... (3 to 7) | Moore's Almanac and Handbook. Sydney, 1853–76. 12mo. | Contains information on all subjects relating to New South Wales. |
| Moore ......... (4) | Spring Life Lyrics. By J. Sheridan Moore. Sydney, 1864. 12mo. | Some of the poems have reference to incidents in the social history of the Colony. |
| Moore ......... (4) | University Reform, its urgency and reasonableness : an Oration. By J. Sheridan Moore. Sydney, 1865. 12mo. Pamph. pp. 23. | Proposes to popularize the University, by affording facilities to young men who cannot attend the Professor's lectures, to become graduates of the University by merely passing the requisite examination ; also, suggests some alterations in and additions to the curriculum. |
| Moore ......... (4.5) | The Newtown Ejectment Case, Doe Dem. Devine *versus* Wilson and others ; with historical introduction, etc., by J. Sheridan Moore. Sydney, 1857. 8vo. Pamph. pp. 127. | Important trial for recovery of property at Newtown fully recorded. |
| Morehead ... (4.7) | Some words for and to the Capitalists and Shareholders in Banks and other moneyed Companies connected with the Colony of New South Wales. By R. A. A. Morehead. Sydney, 1843. 8vo., Pamph., pp. 15. | On the subject of interest charged by Banks and other Institutions for Loans. |
| Mort ......... (3.4) | The question of the Government Guaranteed Railway Shares considered with reference to their being made transferable to bearer, etc, ; with a few remarks pointing out the advantages of Railways over common roads. By T. S. Mort. Sydney, 1854. 8vo. Pamph. pp. 16. | Shows the great advantages likely to accrue from the formation of Railways throughout the Colony, and the best and cheapest means to obtain funds for their extension. |
| Mossman, and Banister. (1 to 4) | Australia visited and revisited. A Narrative of recent Travels and old experiences in Victoria and New South Wales. By Samuel Mossman and Thomas Banister. London, 1853. 8vo. | Contains an excellent and apparently correct description of New South Wales. |
| Mudie ......... (4.5) | The Felony of New South Wales. By J. Mudie. London, 1837. 8vo. | An exaggerated description of the state of society in New South Wales, and full of personalities aroused by the controversies of the day. |

| Mode of Reference. | Full Title, &c. | Remarks. |
|---|---|---|
| Mueller ...... (3) | Definitions of rare or hitherto undescribed Australian Plants. By Dr. Ferdinand Mueller. Melbourne, 1855. 8vo. | An important contribution to the knowledge of Australian Botany. |
| Mundy ...... (4.5) | Our Antipodes; or, Residence and Rambles in the Australian Colonies. By Capt. Mundy. London, 1855. 3 vols. 8vo. | Gives a very fair description of the Colony about the year 1850, the character and pursuits of the inhabitants, &c. |
| Nathan ...... (4) | The Southern Euphrosyne and Australian Miscellany, containing Oriental Moral Tales, Original Anecdotes, Poetry and Music; an historical sketch, with examples of the Native Aboriginal Melodies. By Isaac Nathan. London and Sydney. (n.d.) 4to. | Contains several papers on the Aborigines, and a few of their "corrobory" songs set to music. |
| Neill ......... (3) | The Silkworm; its Education, Reproduction, and Regeneration. By Mrs. Bladen Neill. Melbourne, 1873. 8vo. | Written with the view to promote Sericulture in the Colony. |
| New South Wales. (1 to 7) | The New South Wales Magazine. Sydney, 1833-34. 8vo. | Gives a large mass of interesting historical and social information. |
| New South Wales. (5) | The New South Wales Magazine, or Journal of General Politics, &c., &c. Sydney, 1843. 8vo. | Contains a great deal of useful information on the state of the Colony in 1843. |
| New South Wales. (3.4) | The New South Wales Sporting Magazine. Edited by D. C. F. Scott. Sydney, 1848. 8vo. | In addition to sporting matters, this volume contains valuable information with reference to Australian horses. |
| New South Wales. (3.4) | Northern Agricultural Association, Singleton, New South Wales, Members' Pamphlets, 1870-75. W. Maitland. 8vo. | These reports afford valuable information on all matters relating to live stock and agricultural products, to a late date. |
| New South Wales. (2.4) | The New South Wales Medical Gazette. Sydney, 1871-75. 8vo. | Relates almost entirely to the practice of medicine and surgery. Contains also a paper by Dr. Ross on the climate of Australia. |
| New South Wales. (4.5) | Education v. Religion. Sydney, 1874. 8vo. Pamph. pp. 48. | Opposed to the teaching of religion in the Public Schools, and to the present system of denominational education. |
| New South Wales. (3) | Official Catalogue of the Natural and Industrial Products of New South Wales, forwarded to the International Exhibition of 1876, at Philadelphia. Sydney, 1876. 8vo. | In addition to the list of exhibits, will be found an account of the woods and timber-trees of the Colony, with other information. |
| New South Wales. (5.) | Debate on the Riverine Petition. Melbourne, 1864. 8vo. Pamph. pp. 240. | Speeches in the Legislative Assembly of New South Wales on the proposal to proclaim the Riverine District a Province of New South Wales with special concessions. |

| Mode of Reference. | Full Title, &c. | Remarks. |
|---|---|---|
| New South Wales. (3) | Mines and Mineral Statistics of New South Wales, and Notes on the Geological Collection of the Department of Mines. Compiled by direction of the Hon. John Lucas, M.P., Minister for Mines ; also, Remarks on the Sedimentary Formations of New South Wales, by the Rev. W. B. Clarke, M.A., &c.; and Notes on the Iron and Coal Deposits, Wallerawarg, and on the Diamond Fields, by Professor Liversidge, F.G.S., &c. Sydney, 1875. 8vo. | Contains an immense amount of trustworthy information on the mineral resources and physical structure of New South Wales. |
| New South Wales. (5) | New South Wales Constitution Bill. The Speeches in the Legislative Council of New South Wales, on the second reading of the Bill for framing a new Constitution for the Colony. Edited by E. K. Silvester, Sydney, 1853. 8vo. | A correct report of the debate on the second reading of the Bill to confer a Constitution on the Colony. Many of the speeches are by Mr. Wentworth, and others eminently fitted to express their views on the subject. |
| New South Wales. (3) | The Colony of New South Wales; its Agricultural, Pastoral, and Mining Capabilities. London, 1862. 8vo. Pamph. pp. 16. | A lucid and apparently correct description of the Colony. |
| New South Wales. (3) | The Journal of the Agricultural Society of New South Wales for 1870-1, 1874-7. Sydney. 8vo. | Gives important statistical and other information on the natural productions of the Colony. |
| New South Wales. (4) | Remarks on the probable origin and antiquity of the Aboriginal Natives of New South Wales. By a Colonial Magistrate. Melbourne, 1846. 8vo. Pamph. pp. 40. | Contains much curious information as to the manners and customs of the Aboriginal inhabitants, founded on personal observations and on trustworthy reports of explorers. |
| New South Wales. (3.4) | The Crown Lands Acts, with the Regulations and Forms thereunder; also the Commons Regulation Act. Ninth Edition. Sydney, 1873. 8vo. | A very useful and accurate work on Laws and Regulations relating to the Crown Lands of the Colony. |
| New South Wales. (2 to 7) | The Industrial Progress of New South Wales. Sydney, 1871. 8vo. | Contains a good deal of statistical and other information on the trade, productions, and resources of the Colony. |
| New South Wales. (4.5) | Trial by Jury and a Representative Assembly in New South Wales. Extracted from the Mirror of Parliament. London, 1832. 8vo. Pamph. pp. 38. | Debates in the House of Commons. Shows the estimation in which the Colony was held at that time, by leading politicians in England. |
| New South Wales. (5) | Objections to the project of His Excellency Sir George Gipps, for raising a loan to be secured on the ordinary revenue of the Colony, submitted by His Excellency to the Legislative Council of New South Wales, 1841. Sydney, 1842. Pamph. pp. 20. | This project was to raise by Debentures the sum of £200,000, to be secured on and paid out of the ordinary Revenue, and to be applied to Immigration purposes. |

| Mode of Reference. | Full Title, &c. | Remarks. |
|---|---|---|
| New South Wales. (3.4) | Three years practical experience in New South Wales. Edinburgh, 1838. Pamph. pp. 72. | A favourable view of the prospects and circumstances of the Colony. |
| New South Wales. (4.5) | Clarence and New England Railway League—A synopsis of the proceedings in the agitation for a Line of Railway from the Clarence to New England. Grafton, 1875. 8vo. Pamph. pp. 32. | The league was formed for the purpose of urging the Government to carry out the proposed line, it being considered the most efficient means of securing the trade of the Northern districts, "now being rapidly attracted by Queensland." |
| New South Wales. (4.5) | The Causes of the Former Prosperity and Present State of the Colony of New South Wales. Sydney, ca. 1845. Pamph. pp. 12. | Gives as first causes of prosperity, free grants of land to capitalists and abundant labour (convict). Depression as caused by the rise in price of waste lands, and the introduction of free immigrants without capital. |
| New South Wales. (4.5) | Observations on the proposed New Constitution for New South Wales, by an Old Colonist. Sydney, 1852. 12mo. Pamph. pp. 16. | A statement of the objects to be attained by the formation of a second or Upper Chamber, and makes suggestions as to its composition. |
| New South Wales. (4.5) | Illustrations of the Present State and Future Prospects of New South Wales, by an Impartial Observer. Sydney, 1835. Pamph. pp. 70. | Historical review. Granting of land. Evils of a bad system of female immigration. Punishments, &c. |
| New South Wales. (4.5) | Report of the Debate in the Legislative Council of New South Wales, on the Division of the Territory, and the introduction of a New System for the disposal of Crown Lands. Sydney, 1840. Pamph. pp. 41 and Appendix. | Most important document, full of statistical information. Regulations for sale of Crown Lands, &c. All the Speakers opposed to dismemberment. |
| New South Wales. (4.5) | Report of the Proceedings and Financial State of the Association, &c., &c., designated the New South Wales Association for preventing the revival of Transportation; with Appendices and Supplement. Sydney, 1851. 8vo. Pamph. pp. 64. | A small but influential body of Colonists found assigned labour extremely profitable, and endeavoured to secure a continuance of transportation, but the bulk of the population was altogether averse to it. |
| Norton ...... (1.4) | Port Jackson and the City of Sydney, by James Norton. Sydney, 1853. 8vo. Pamph. | A short essay, faithfully describing the aspects of the City and its neighbourhood. |
| Norton ...... (4.5) | The Condition of the Colony of New South Wales, by the Honorable James Norton. Sydney, 1860. 8vo. Pamph. pp. 16. | Describes the Colony at a period of depression. Advocates protection to local industries. Refers to the unsatisfactory state of education. |
| Norton ...... (4.5) | Essays and Reflections in Australia, by a Layman (James Norton). Sydney, 1853. 8vo. Pamph. pp. 106. | Contains some remarks on the Constitution of New South Wales, on railways, and other matters. |
| O'Hara ...... (3.4.5) | History of New South Wales. (By O'Hara.) London, 1817. 8vo. | A careful compilation. The writer has confined himself to leading historical facts and social events, from the foundation of the Colony to about 1817. |

| Mode of Reference. | Full Title, &c. | Remarks. |
|---|---|---|
| O'Shaughnessey. (3.4.5) | Australian Almanack and Sydney Directory. Compiled by E. W. O'Shaughnessey. Sydney, 1833-35. 8vo. | Full of general information. Contains a Chronological Table of noteworthy occurrences, from the foundation of the Colony to 1832. |
| Oxley ......... (1.3.5) | Journals of two Expeditions into the interior of New South Wales, 1817-18. By J. Oxley. London, 1820. 4to. | Represents an important step in the progress of exploration; but the author erroneously concluded that the interior of the Colony was an immense swamp. |
| Page............ (3.4) | The Clarence, New England, and Gwydir Almanac and Gazetteer. Published by Thomas Page, Grafton, 1871-72. 12mo. | Affords useful statistical information. |
| Palmer ...... (4.5) | Kidnapping in the South Seas, being a narrative of a three months' cruise of H.M.S. "Rosario." By Capt. Geo. Palmer, R.N. Edinburgh, 1871, 8vo. | Gives an account of the trial of the "Daphne" in the Vice-Admiralty Court of New South Wales, and describes the scene at the Water Police Court, Sydney. |
| Paris ......... (3) | Exposition Universelle de 1867, Nouvelle Galles du Sud, Australie. Paris, 1867. 8vo. Pamph. pp. 47. | The Catalogue of Exhibits contributed by New South Wales to the Paris Exhibition. Contains several papers on the capabilities and statistics of the Colony. |
| Parkes......... (5) | Speeches from 1849 to 1874. By Henry Parkes. Melbourne, 1876. 8vo. | "As the debates in which these speeches were delivered, and the events out of which the platform addresses arose, belong to the political history of the Colony, this volume constitutes a really acceptable contribution to that history."—*Melbourne Argus.* |
| Parkes......... (3.4.5) | The Mother of the Australias: a Lecture, by Henry Parkes. London, 1862. 12mo. Pamph. pp. 15. | A short but correct account of New South Wales to about 1860. |
| Parkes......... (4.5) | The Electoral Act and how to work it. A series of letters on the subject of the approaching Elections. By Henry Parkes. Sydney, 1859. 8vo. Pamph. pp. 20. | The object of these letters was to effect a reform in the electoral system of the Colony. |
| Parkes......... (4.5) | Murmurs of the Stream. By Henry Parkes. Sydney, 1857. 12mo. Stolen Moments. A short series of Poems. By Henry Parkes. Sydney. 1842. 12mo. | These collections consist of short lyrical pieces, and political and other poems. Many are descriptive of Colonial life and events. |
| Peisley......... (4.5) | A brief Memoir of John Peisley the notorious bushranger, with a full report of his trial and condemnation for the wilful murder of William Benyen. Bathurst, 1862. Pamph. 12mo., pp. 31. | Part of a painful chapter in the history of New South Wales, when for a time a band of murderers set the police at defiance. |
| Peppercorne.. (1.2) | The Rivers of Australia. Published in the Magazine of Science and Art, by F. S. Peppercorne, C.E. Sydney, 1858. pp. 4. | A very instructive paper on the River Systems of Australia. |

| Mode of Reference. | Full Title, &c. | Remarks. |
|---|---|---|
| Peppercorne.. (1.2.3) | Memoir relative to the Improvement of Harbours and Rivers in Australia, with incidental remarks on Canals and Railways. By Frederick S. Peppercorne. Sydney, 1856. 8vo. Pamph., pp. 31. | The writer shows that the conformation of Australia is specially adapted to the formation of canals. |
| Peron ......... (1.5) | Voyage de Découvertes aux Terres Australes sur les Corvettes le Géographe, le Naturaliste, et la Göelette le Casuarina, pendant les années 1800–4. Par. F. Peron et L. Freycinet. Paris, 1807–16. 2 vols. 4to. Cartes, roy. 4to. | That portion of the work which refers to New South Wales gives an apparently truthful description of Port Jackson, the City of Sydney, its institutions, &c., about the year 1802. |
| Petitions...... (4.5.6) | Report of the Proceedings of the General Meeting of the supporters of the Petitions to His Majesty and the House of Commons, from Members of Council, Magistrates, Clergy, Landholders, Merchants, and other Free Inhabitants of New South Wales, held at the Committee Rooms, George Street, Sydney, 30th May, 1836. Sydney, 1836. 8vo. Pamph. pp. 51. | The petitions urge the necessity for devoting the revenue derived from Land Sales to the purposes of immigration, the consolidation of the laws, modification of judicial regulations, and improved system of police. They protest against the Jury Act, which gives to convicts whose sentences have expired the privilege of acting as jurors, &c., &c. |
| Phillip ...... (5) | The Voyage of Governor Phillip to Botany Bay. By A. Phillip. London, 1789. 4to. | An authentic and ample account of the first expedition to New South Wales, and settlement of the Colony, in 1788. |
| Pidgeon ...... (4) | The Life, Experience, and Journal of Nathaniel Pidgeon, City Missionary; written by himself. Sydney, 1857. 12mo. | Throws some light on the habits of the poorer classes in Sydney, about the year 1850. |
| Pilorgerie ... (3.4.5) | Histoire de Botany Bay. Par Jules de la Pilorgerie. Paris, 1836. 8vo. | An interesting sketch; apparently compiled from the works of English writers. |
| Plunkett...... (4) | The Australian Magistrate; or a Guide to the duties of a Justice of the Peace for the Colony of New South Wales. Also a brief summary of the Law of Landlord and Tenant. By J. Hubert Plunkett, A.B. Sydney, 1835. 8vo. | A digest of the laws in force in the Colony, carefully abbreviated and arranged. |
| Plunkett ...... (4) | The foregoing, corrected and enlarged. By W. H. Wilkinson. Sydney, 1866. 8vo. | Considerable additions made to the original work, and many of the cases decided in the Supreme Court given. Also forms used for various legal purposes. |
| Polding ...... (4.5) | An Answer to the Letter addressed to the Lord Bishop of Australia in defence of the Most Rev. Dr. Polding's usurpation of the title and dignity of Archbishop of Sydney, and Metropolitan of New Holland. By a Layman. Sydney, 8vo. Pamph. pp. 20. | Religious Controversy. |

| Mode of Reference. | Full Title, &c. | Remarks. |
|---|---|---|
| Polehampton (4) | Kangaroo Land. By the Rev. A. Polehampton. London, 1862. 12mo. | Gives a truthful picture of Colonial life. |
| Port Phillip.. (3.5.7) | A Report, Commercial, Statistical, and General, on the District of Port Phillip, New South Wales, for the Half-year ended 31 July, 1846. Melbourne, 1846. 8vo. Pamph. pp. 40. | At the time this report was issued the Colony of Victoria had not been separated from New South Wales. The separation occurred in 1857. |
| Powell ...... (2.3.4) | New Homes for the Old Country. By George S. Baden-Powell. London, 1872. 8vo. | That part which refers to New South Wales gives a tolerably faithful description of the colonists, climate, productions, &c., at the present time. |
| Pridden ...... (4.5) | Australia, its History and Present Condition. By the Rev. W. Pridden, M.A. London, 1843. 12mo. | Carefully compiled from trustworthy sources, and treats of the early history of the Colony, manners and customs of the colonists and aboriginal inhabitants, &c. |
| Protection ... (3.7) | The Policy of Protection economically and morally considered, with reference in particular to Colonial Industry. Sydney, 1868. 8vo. Pamph. 18 pp. | A treatise in favour of Protection to Colonial Industries. |
| Prout ......... (4.5) | Sydney Illustrated, by J. S. Prout; with letter-press description, by J. Rae, M.A. Sydney, 1844. Fol. | An excellent description of the City of Sydney and Suburbs, about the year 1843. |
| Prout ......... (4.5) | Memoirs of the life of the Rev. John Williams, Missionary to Polynesia. By Ebenezer Prout. London, 1843. | Describes the Rev. J. Williams' visits to New South Wales, and indicates the relation of the Colony to the Islands of the Pacific. |
| Rae ............ (4) | Gleanings from my Scrap Book. By John Rae, A.M. 2 vols. 8vo. Sydney, 1869. | Contains a humourous and sprightly description, in verse, of the Mayor's Fancy Ball, and other social sketches. |
| Rae ............ (1.3.4.) | Railways of New South Wales; their construction and working, from 1872 to 1875 inclusive. By John Rae, A.M., Commissioner for Railways. Sydney, 1877. fol. | Full of trustworthy information on everything relating to the Railways of the Colony, with explanatory diagrams and maps. |
| Ragged School. (4) | Reports of the Sussex-street Ragged and Industrial School. 12mo. Pamphs. 1861-76. | Inaugurated 1860. |
| Ranken ...... (2 to 7) | The Dominion of Australia. An account of its foundations. By W. H. L. Ranken. London, 1874. 8vo. | For information, this work is most valuable; it gives a survey of the past and present state of the Colony; refers to the climate, productive properties of the soil, the mineral resources, &c. |

| Mode of Reference. | Full Title, &c. | Remarks. |
|---|---|---|
| Ranken ...... (3.4.5) | Bush Essays. By Capricornus. Edinburgh, 1872. 8vo. Pamph. pp. 47. The Squatting System of Australia. By Capricornus (George Ranken). Edinburgh, 1875. 8vo. Pamph. pp. 31. Colonization in 1876. By Capricornus. Sydney, 1876. 8vo. Pamph. pp. 39. Homestead Settlement. Grazing, Past, Present, and Future. By Capricornus. Sydney, 1877, 8vo. Pamph. pp. 45. | These papers, besides other valuable information, give a general sketch of the history of the Colony, and throw a great deal of light on the origin and progress of the squatting system in Australia. |
| Raymond ... (3) | The New South Wales Calendar and General Post Office Directory. Compiled by James Raymond. Sydney, 1832–37. 8vo. | Contains a good deal of information on trade, land regulations, &c. |
| Reid............ (3.4.5.) | Two Voyages to New South Wales, &c. By T. Reid. London, 1822. 8vo. | Gives apparently a faithful account of the Colony, as a convict settlement, including facts and observations relative to the management and conduct of the convicts. |
| Reid............ (5) | The Diplomacy of Victoria on the Postal Question, and the true Policy of New South Wales. By G. H. Reid. Sydney, 1873. 8vo. pp. 14. | Refers to the steps taken by the Government of the Colony of Victoria to secure to itself the Ocean Mail Service between Australia and Point de Galle. |
| Reid............ (3) | Five Free Trade Essays. Inscribed to the Electors of Victoria. By Geo. H. Reid. Melbourne, 1875. 8vo. | These Essays throw light upon the present position and the free-trade policy of New South Wales, and are well worth perusal. |
| Reid............ (1 to 7) | An Essay on New South Wales, the Mother Colony of the Australias. By G. H. Reid. Sydney, 1876. Roy. 8vo. | Full of information on all subjects pertaining to the Colony, compiled from official and authentic documents. |
| Ridley ......... (4) | Kamilaroi and other Australian Languages. By the Rev. W. Ridley, M.A. Sydney, 1875. Roy. 8vo. | The dialects of the various tribes inhabiting Australia. A valuable contribution to the science of Philology. |
| Rifle Association. (4.5) | Reports of the New South Wales Rifle Association. 1861–76. 8vo. | Instituted 5th October, 1860. Account of Matches, etc., etc. Sustained by private subscription and Government grant of £200 per annum. |
| Rigg............ (4.5) | A Digest of the Laws and Regulations of the Australian Wesleyan Connection. By Chas. W. Rigg, Wesleyan Minister. Sydney, 1863. 12mo. | Gives authentic facts relating to the Wesleyan Church in New South Wales. |
| Ritchie......... (5) | The British World in the East.—A Guide Historical, Moral, and Commercial, to India, China, Australia, etc. By Leitch Ritchie. London, 1847. 2 vols. 8vo. | Contains a few chapters detailing facts in the early history of the Colony. Statistics for 1843. |

| Mode of Reference. | Full Title, &c. | Remarks. |
|---|---|---|
| Robinson ...... (1 to 7) | New South Wales, the oldest and richest of the Australian Colonies. By Charles Robinson. Sydney, 1873. 8vo. | An accurate description of New South Wales; its pastoral and mineral wealth and resources, manufacturing industries, &c. |
| Robinson...... (1 to 7) | The Progress and Resources of New South Wales. By Chas. Robinson, Sydney, 1877. 8vo. Pamph. pp. 25. | Compiled at the close of the International Exhibition, held at Philadelphia, by the Secretary to the Commission. Gives a short but excellent description of the Colony. |
| Robison ...... (5) | A short statement of the case of R. Robison, Esq., late Captain of the New South Wales Veteran Companies, as brought forward in the House of Commons by Dr. Lushington, on 11th July, 1833. The sentence of the Court Martial against him on the charges of Lieut.-General Ralph Darling, and other documents. London, 1834. 8vo. A letter addressed by R. Robison to the Members of the House of Commons, containing an outline of Evidence against Lieut.-General Darling, late Governor of N. S. W., in reply to a pamphlet privately circulated among them by that officer. London, 1835. 8vo. | Robison accuses Governor Darling (q. v.) of gross maladministration of justice, of cruelty to prisoners, and of other unlawful acts. Having tried on the irons used for the punishment of Sudds and Thompson, and made remarks upon them which were reported to the Governor, he was brought to trial, and, by the undue influence of the Governor sentence was recorded against him. |
| Rolleston ... (3.4.5) | Statistical Review of the Progress of New South Wales during the last ten years. By Christopher Rolleston. Sydney, 1873. 8vo. Pamph. pp. 19. | A trustworthy source of information on the population, productions, trade and commerce of the Colony. |
| Ross............ (4) | Jottings on Vitality; or, the Physical Basis of Life. By Andrew Ross, M.D. Sydney, 1872. 8vo. Pamph. pp. 31. | Throws some light on the social and political state of the Colony. |
| Ross............ (4) | Power of Mind over Matter. By Andrew Ross, M.D. Sydney, 1872. 8vo. Pamph. pp. 23. | Refers principally to two murders committed on the Parramatta River, and to the want of sound moral training. |
| Rowcroft...... (4) | An Emigrant in search of a Colony. By Charles Rowcroft. London, 1851. 12mo. | The descriptions of a "Boiling-down," and of the scenery of the Blue Mountains are, on the whole, accurate. |
| Royal Society (3.4) | Transactions of the (Philosophical) Royal Society of New South Wales. 1862-75. Sydney. 8vo. | Contains several valuable papers on subjects of interest relating to the Colony. |
| Russell........ (2) | Results of Meteorological Observations made in New South Wales, under the direction of H. C. Russell, B.A., &c., Government Astronomer. Sydney, 1870-75. Roy. 8vo. | A trustworthy report up to the end of 1869, and from thence to 1875; with remarks on the climate. |
| Russell ...... (2) | Climate of New South Wales: Descriptive, Historical, and Tabular. By H. C. Russell, B.A., &c. Sydney, 1877. Roy. 8vo. | The most complete work of reference devoted to the subject yet published. |

| Mode of Reference. | Full Title, &c. | Remarks. |
|---|---|---|
| Sailors' Home (4) | Reports of the Sydney Sailors' Home, N.S.W. Sydney. 12mo. | Instituted 1862. |
| St. Paul's ..... (4.5) | The origin and foundation of St. Paul's College, established within the University of Sydney, and incorporated by Act of the Legislature, 1855. Sydney, 1856. 8vo. Pamph. pp. 27. By-laws and Statutes of and relating to St. Paul's College, within the University of Sydney, with some account of its Foundation. Sydney, 1863. 12mo. Pamph. pp. 38. | One of the affiliated Colleges connected with the University of Sydney. Episcopalian. |
| St. Andrew's.. (4) | Report of the Committee of Trustees for the erection of Saint Andrew's Scots' Church, Sydney, 1837. 8vo. Pamph. pp. 15. | First Pastor, Rev. J. M'Garvie. First steps taken 18th Nov., 1832. |
| St. Andrew's.. (4.5) | Report of the Building Committee of St. Andrew's Cathedral, Sydney. For 1857. 8vo. Pamph. pp. 12. | The foundation stone of the Cathedral was laid in 1832. |
| St. Julian ..... (3) | Productions and Resources of New South Wales. By C. St. Julian and E. K. Silvester. Sydney, 1857. 12mo. | A carefully-written work on the Natural History, Botany, and Statistics of the Colony. |
| Sands .......... (3.4) | Sands' Sydney and Suburban Directory, 1858–76. Sydney. 8vo. | In addition to the street and business directory, this work gives a list of Government and other Colonial Institutions, besides a good deal of useful information. |
| School ......... (4.5) | Reports of the Committee of the Sydney School of Industry. Sydney. | Instituted 1826. Managed by a Ladies' Committee for the education of 20 girls. |
| Scott ......... (3) | Australian Lepidoptera and their Transformations. Drawn from life, by Harriett and Helena Scott; with descriptions general and systematic, by A. W. Scott, M.A. Parts 1, 2, & 3. Folio. London, 1864. *Mammalia, Recent + extinct.* | Valuable contribution to the entomological Natural History of the Colony. |
| Settlers and Convicts. (4.5) | Settlers and Convicts, or Recollections of sixteen years labour in the Australian Backwoods. By an Australian Mechanic. London, 1847. 12mo. | The sketches of bush life in the earlier days of the Colony, with the various incidents narrated, are very interesting, and without doubt truthful. |
| Shaw ......... (4) | "Typical Australians." A Lecture. By Mr. J. Shaw, of the Yass Grammar School. Yass, 1872. 8vo. Pamph. pp. 11. | An amusing description of different phases of character to be met with in the Colony. |
| Shaw ......... (4.5) | Tramp to the Diggings; being notes of a ramble in Australia and New Zealand. By John Shaw, M.D. London, 1852. 12mo. | Describes Sydney during the excitement caused by the discovery of gold; also the roads of the Colony, and its politics and statesmen. |

| Mode of Reference. | Full Title, &c. | Remarks. |
|---|---|---|
| Shepherd...... (3) | Lectures on the Horticulture of New South Wales. By Thomas Shepherd. Sydney, 1835. 8vo. | Throws some light on the suitableness of the climate for the production of vegetables and fruit. |
| Sherriff ...... (3.4) | The Australian Almanac for 1865 to 1877. Published by J. L. Sherriff. Sydney, 12mo. | Contains Statistical Returns, Country Directory, and other useful information. |
| Sidney......... (2 to 7) | The Three Colonies of Australia. By Samuel Sidney. London, 1852. 8vo. | That part which relates to New South Wales, both historical and descriptive, gives a short but very correct account of the Colony to about 1852. |
| Silver ......... (2 to 7) | Silver's Guide to Australia. London, 1863. 8vo. | The small portion which refers to New South Wales gives a correct description of the Colony. |
| Silvester ...... (4.5) | New South Wales Constitution Bill. The Speeches in the Legislative Council of New South Wales on the second reading of the Bill for framing a new Constitution for the Colony. Edited by E. K. Silvester. Sydney, 1853. 8vo. | A valuable record of the political progress of the Colony, and of the oratory of its leading men. |
| Smiles ......... (4) | A Boy's Voyage round the World. Edited by S. Smiles. London, 1872. 12mo. | Contains a brief account of Sydney. |
| Smith ......... (4) | The Law List, 1873, comprising the Judges and Officers of the different Courts of Justice, Counsel, Attorneys, Notaries, &c., in Victoria, New South Wales, &c. By R. H. Smith. 12mo. Melbourne, 1873. | Gives a large amount of legal information. |
| South Asian Register. (4.5) | South Asian Register, December, 1828. Sydney. 8vo. | Gives a description of the Colony in 1828; also, a curious sketch of Sydney life as it then appeared. |
| Southey ...... (2.3.5) | The Rise, Progress, and Present State of Colonial Wools, comprising those of Australia, Van Diemen's Land, New Zealand, &c., &c. By Thos. Southey. London, 1848. 8vo. | Traces the various steps taken for the introduction of the merino sheep into the Colony ; its influence on the prosperity of New South Wales ; with statistics showing the rapid increase of the flocks, and the suitability of the climate for their propagation. |
| Stamer......... (4) | The Gentleman Emigrant. By W. Stamer. 2 vols. 8vo. London, 1874. | The last half of the first volume relates almost entirely to Australian bush life, of which it gives a lively and fairly truthful description. |
| Stephen ...... (4) | Constitution, Rules, and Practice of the Supreme Court of New South Wales. By Alfred Stephen, Esq. Sydney, 1843-5. 8vo. | This compilation was the work of His Honor Sir Alfred Stephen, late Chief Justice of the Colony, and is of much practical value. |
| Stephen ...... (4.5) | Electoral Bill. Speech of Sir Alfred Stephen, Knt., in the Legislative Council of N.S.W., on the second reading of the Bill to amend the Electoral Law. Sydney, 1858. 8vo. Pamph. pp. 38. | Against universal suffrage, favourable to vote by ballot, and to a property qualification for voters. |

| Mode of Reference. | Full Title, &c. | Remarks. |
|---|---|---|
| Stephen ...... (4.5) | Thoughts on the Constitution of a second Legislative Chamber for New South Wales, in a letter to the Attorney General. By Sir Alfred Stephen, Knt., Chief Justice. Sydney, 1853. 8vo. Pamph. pp. 20. | Reviews the several proposals for the Constitution of a Second or Upper Chamber, and suggests that it be composed of 25 Members, viz., the Chief Justice for the time being, 12 Members nominated by the Governor to hold their seats for life, and 12 elected by the Assembly for nine years. |
| Stephen ...... (4.5) | Appendix to "Thoughts on the Legislative Constitution of New South Wales." By Sir A. Stephen, Knt., Chief Justice. Sydney, 1853. 8vo. Pamph. pp. 7. | Enforces his views previously expressed by comparing his proposition with the Upper House of Canada. |
| Stokes ......... (1.5) | Discoveries in Australia, with an account of the coasts and rivers explored and surveyed during the voyage of H.M.S. "Beagle," in the years 1837–43. By Captain J. L. Stokes, R.N. London, 1846. 2 vols. 8vo. | A most important work, and contains a large mass of information concerning New South Wales. |
| Stow ......... (4) | Conference of Congregational Independents. Congregationalism in the Colonies. By the Rev. T. Q. Stow. Sydney, 1855. 8vo. Pamph. pp. 27. | Address delivered to Ministers and Delegates assembled from the four Colonies of N.S. Wales, Victoria, S. Australia, and Tasmania. |
| Strzelecki ... (1.2.3) | Physical Description of New South Wales, &c. By P. E. de Strzelecki. London, 1845. 8vo. | A valuable work — relates to Colonial agriculture, climate, &c. |
| Sturt ......... (1 to 5) | Two Expeditions into the Interior of Southern Australia during the years 1828, 1829, 1830, 1831, with observations on the soil, climate, and general resources of the Colony of New South Wales. By Captain C. Sturt. 2 vols. 8vo. London, 1833. | Full of information on the physical structure, soil, climate, and productions of the Colony. |
| Suttor ......... (3.4) | The Public Lands—progressive purchase, fixed price, mixed farming, homestead villages. By Edwin C. Suttor. Sydney, 1871. 12mo. Pamph. pp. 18. | The object of this pamphlet is to urge an alteration in the existing laws relating to the sale or other disposal of the public lands in the Colony, and to show the necessity of devising some means by which the population may be increased. |
| Sydney ...... (4) | Inaugural Address, delivered on the opening of the University of Sydney, Monday, October 11th, 1852. By the Hon. Sir Charles Nicholson, Vice-Provost, and the Rev. J. Woolley, D.C.L. Sydney, 1852. 4to. pp. 32. | Gives an account of the ceremony of inauguration. |
| Sydney Gazette ... (1 to 8) | The Sydney Gazette and New South Wales Advertiser. Published by authority. Sydney, 1803–42. Fol. | The only record of current events, in the early days of the Colony, extant. |

D

| Mode of Reference. | Full Title, &c. | Remarks. |
|---|---|---|
| Sydney ...... (4) | Reports of the Sydney Infirmary and Dispensary—1844 to 1876. 8vo. Pamphs. | Instituted in the year 1844. A most valuable Institution, supported by grants from Government and voluntary subscriptions. |
| Sydney ...... (3) | Sydney General Trade List. Compiled weekly, under the authority of the Customs. Sydney, 1828–31. 4to. | Gives prices current, or value of merchandise, &c., during 1828-30. Rates of insurance, exchange, and freight. |
| Sydney......... (4) | Reports of the Sydney Bethel Union —1842-76. | Instituted as a sailors' mission. |
| Sydney ...... (4.5) | Reports of the Sydney College in New South Wales, with a short statement of the proceedings of the Committee of Management. Sydney, 1835. 8vo. Pamph., pp. 16. | Established 1830. |
| Sydney ...... (4) | The Sydney University Calendar. Sydney, 1852-76. 8vo. | Contains the By-laws and Acts relating to the University, table of fees, &c. |
| Sydney ...... (4) | Vice and its Victims in Sydney; the cause and cure. By a pupil of the late Professor John Woolley, D.C.L., Principal of Sydney University. Sydney, 1873. 8vo. Pamph., pp. 77. | A comment on the state of public morality in Sydney. |
| Tebbutt ...... (2) | Meteorological Observations made at the private Observatory of John Tebbutt, the Peninsular, Windsor, New South Wales, in the years 1863-70. By John Tebbutt, F.R.A.S. Sydney, 1868, 1874. Roy. 8vo. and fol. | A record of daily observations taken at Windsor. The tables are well arranged, and contain valuable information respecting the weather, climate, &c. |
| Tegg ......... (3.4) | Tegg's New South Wales Pocket Almanack and Remembrancer. Sydney, 1837-44. 12mo. | Does not contain much information that is likely to be useful at the present day. |
| Tench ......... (4.5) | A Narrative of the Expedition to Botany Bay, with an account of New South Wales. Third edition. By Captain Watkin Tench. London, 1789. 8vo. | The author sailed with the first fleet to found an establishment at Botany Bay. The book gives an interesting and trustworthy account of the proceedings, also of the state of the Colony to the end of the year 1788. |
| Tench ......... (2.3.4.5) | A complete account of the Settlement at Port Jackson. By Captain Watkin Tench. London, 1793. 4to. | A chronicle of events from 1788 to 1791. Contains useful information as to climate, productions, inhabitants, &c. |
| Therry......... (4.5) | An appeal on behalf of the Roman Catholics of N.S.W., in a letter to Edward Blount, Esq., M.P. for Steyning, from Roger Therry, Esq., occasioned by letters addressed to him by Captain Sir Edward Parry, R.N., and the Venerable Archdeacon Broughton. Sydney, 1833. Pamph., pp. 50. | Refers to the subscriptions which were solicited towards the completion of the Roman Catholic chapel. The Archdeacon, it appears in his letter, stated that the Protestant inhabitants of the Colony could not "subscribe to build a Roman Catholic chapel, without guilt." |

| Mode of Reference. | Full Title, &c. | Remarks. |
|---|---|---|
| Therry ......... (3.4.5) | Reminiscences of Thirty years' residence in New South Wales and Victoria. By Roger Therry. London, 1863. 8vo. | Written by a late Judge of the Supreme Court. Contains a good deal of curious information relating to the criminal population and colonial society from 1829 to 1859. |
| Therry ......... (4.5) | Letter to the Right Hon. W. E. Gladstone, Esq., M.P., with the address to the Jury at the opening of the first Circuit Court at Brisbane, Moreton Bay, May 13th, 1850, and Speech at the Dinner given to the Judge and Members of the Circuit by the Magistracy and Gentry of the District. By His Honor Mr. Justice Therry. Sydney, 1850. 8vo. | A number of horrible cases cited to show the necessity for stringent and exemplary punishment of criminals. |
| Thompson ... (5) | Report of the Proceedings of the National Banquet held at the Prince of Wales Theatre, Sydney, on the 17th July, 1856, to celebrate the establishment and inauguration of Responsible Government in the Colony of New South Wales. Edited by Richard Thompson. Sydney, 1856. 8vo. Pamph., pp. 45. | "A festival most satisfactory in the demeanour and speeches of those present." |
| Thomson ...... (4.5) | Corrected Report of the Speeches of the Hon. Edward Deas Thomson, Esq., Colonial Secretary of N.S.W., on the first and second reading of the Bill for the division of the Colony into Electoral Districts. Sydney, 1851. 8vo. Pamph., pp. 47. | Shows that the Bill in question was not framed for the protection of any particular interest, but was based on the principles of property and population combined. Contains statistical statement of stock and population. |
| Threlkeld ..... (4) | An Australian Grammar, comprehending the Principles and natural Rules of the Language, as spoken by the Aborigines of New South Wales. By L. E. Threlkeld. Sydney, 1834. 8vo. A Key to the structure of the Language spoken by the Aborigines of New South Wales. By L. E. Threlkeld. Sydney, 1850. 8vo. | A curious and, on the whole, a correct analysis of the dialect spoken by the Aboriginal inhabitants. |
| Tompson ...... (4.5) | Wild Notes from the Lyre of a Native Minstrel. By Chas. Tompson, junr. Sydney, 1826. 4to. | A volume of Australian Poems. Contains an elegy on the death of Governor Macquarie, and lines on the anniversary of the colonization of New South Wales. |
| Torrens ........ (5) | The South Australian System of Conveyance by Registration of Title. Adelaide, 1859. Post 8vo. | The principle of transferring landed property by registration of title was introduced into the Colony of N.S.W. with most beneficial results, and is known as "Torrens' Act." |

| Mode of Reference. | Full Title, &c. | Remarks |
|---|---|---|
| Townsend..... (3.4) | Rambles and Observations in New South Wales. By P. J. Townsend. London, 1849. 12mo. | Gives a truthful account of the agricultural capabilities and products of the Colony, the character and pursuits of the inhabitants, etc. |
| Transportation. (4) | A letter addressed to the Squatters of New South Wales on the Transportation and Labour Questions. By a Squatter. Sydney, 1851. 8vo. Pamph. pp. 16. | Opposed to a revival of transportation; advises the assisted immigration of people with families. |
| Transportation. (4.5) | Report of the Proceedings and Financial State of the Association formed at a great public meeting of the inhabitants of the Colony, etc., etc., designated the N. S. W. Association for preventing the revival of Transportation. Sydney, 1851. 8vo. Pamph. pp. 64. | Important, as giving the views of some of the leading men of the Colony on the subject of transportation. |
| Trollope....... (3.4.5) | Australia and New Zealand. By Anthony Trollope. London, 1873. 2 vols. 8vo. | That part relating to New South Wales gives an accurate description of the pursuits and manners of the Colonists, together with a general sketch of the history and resources of the Colony. |
| Turnbull...... (4.5) | Voyage round the World in the years 1800 to 1804, in which the Author visits the English settlements of Botany Bay, etc. By John Turnbull. London, 1813. 4to. | Gives a short account of New South Wales, and of the habits of the Aborigines, in the early days of colonisation. |
| Tyerman ...... (4) | A Plea for Freethinkers: being a letter to the Right Rev. Frederick Barker, D.D., Lord Bishop of Sydney, By John Tyerman. Sydney, 1875. 12mo. Pamph. pp. 11. | This refers to an address delivered by the Bishop of Sydney at the annual meeting of the New South Wales Association for the Promotion of Morality, on which occasion, it appears, he made some allusion to Mr. T. as an "infidel lecturer." |
| Tyrrell......... (4.5) | Remarks on the Third Report of the Board of National Education in N. S. W. for 1850. By the Right Rev. the Lord Bishop of Newcastle. Sydney 1851. 8vo. Pamph. pp. 27. | Condemnatory of the National System, and advocating the Denominational. |
| Ullathorne ... (4) | A few words to the Rev. H. Fulton and his readers, with a glance at the Archdeacon, from the Rev. W. B. Ullathorne, C.V.G. Sydney, 1833. 8vo. Pamph. pp. 56. | A reply to pamphlets written by the Rev. H. Fulton and Archdeacon Broughton on religious subjects. |
| Ullathorne ... (4.5) | A reply to Judge Burton, of the Supreme Court of N.S.W., on "The State of Religion" in the Colony. By the Rev. W. B. Ullathorne, C.V.G., Sydney, 1840. 8vo. | An exposition of Roman Catholic operations in the Colony at that date, with much statistical information. |

| Mode of Reference. | Full Title, &c. | Remarks. |
|---|---|---|
| Vanderkiste... (4) | Lost, but not for ever. My personal narrative of starvation and providence in the Australian Mountain Regions. By the Rev. R. W. Vanderkiste. London. 8vo. 1863. | Contains a number of incidents of Australian bush life, and religious reflections thereon. |
| Vaughan ...... (4) | Advent Conferences. By Archbishop Vaughan. Sydney, 1876. 8vo. | Written in defence of the Roman Catholic Faith, in consequence of the attack, alleged to have been made by the Bishop of Sydney, in his speech when laying the foundation stone of the Protestant Hall, Sydney. |
| Vicars ......... (3.4.) | The Tariff, Immigration, and the Labour Question, discussed by John Vicars, Tweed Factory. Sydney, 1877. 8vo. Pamph. pp. 20. | In favour of protection to native industries and opposed to assisted immigration. |
| Vineyards ... (3.4) | Report of the Hunter River Vineyard Association. Sydney, 1854. 8vo. Pamph. pp. 55. | The papers written by the various Vinegrowers contain most valuable information, in reference to the soil, aspect, and culture best adapted for Vines in this Colony. |
| Wakefield ... (4.5) | A letter from Sydney. (By E. G. Wakefield.) Edited by R. Gouger, London, 1829. 12mo. | Relates principally to the state of society in Sydney, and is evidently a prejudiced account. |
| Walker ...... (4.5) | The Flood in the Hawkesbury. By W. Walker, July, 1850. 4to. | A short poem, descriptive of the great Flood in the Hawkesbury District. |
| Walker ...... (4.5) | Australian Literature. A lecture delivered at the Windsor School of Arts, on the evening of Wednesday, 20th July, 1864. By William Walker, Esq., M.L.A., President of the Institution. Sydney, 1864. 8vo. Pamph. pp. 31. | Interesting and instructive review of the early publications of the Colony, and its leading literary works. |
| Wall ......... (3) | History and description of the Skeleton of a new Sperm Whale lately set up in the Australian Museum. By William S. Wall. Sydney, 8vo. 1851. | Refers to two new species of the Sperm Whale found off the Coast of New South Wales. |
| Wallis ......... (5) | An Historical Account of the Colony of New South Wales and its dependent Settlements. Illustrated with twelve Views engraved by W. Preston. Folio. London, 1821. | Not in the Free Public Library. No reference to be found. |
| Wardley ...... (4) | Some Phases of Insanity and its treatment popularly considered. By E. Wardley, M.R.C.S.L. Sydney. 8vo. Pamph. pp. 38. | Partly refers to some of the causes of insanity in New South Wales. |
| Waugh ...... (4.5) | Waugh and Cox's Directory of Sydney and its Suburbs for 1855. Sydney. 8vo. | Does not contain information likely to be useful, with the exception of an explanation of the boundaries of the city of Sydney, its wards and parishes. |

| Mode of Reference. | Full Title, &c. | Remarks. |
|---|---|---|
| Waugh ...... (3) | Australian Settler's Handbook. By J. W. Waugh. Sydney, 1861. | Practical hints for the inexperienced on the most simple and practical way of cultivating and improving their land. Contains much useful matter. |
| Waugh ...... (2.3.5) | Waugh's Australian Almanac. Sydney, 1858–6k. 12mo. | Full of useful information, and contains valuable data concerning the climate of Australia. |
| Waugh and Cox ......... (3) | Waugh and Cox's Australian Almanac. Sydney, 1855–57. 12mo. | Contains, in addition to some useful information, remarks on the pastoral resources of Australia, and on Australian wine. |
| Welch ......... (4.5) | Convict and Free Labour for New South Wales. By R. P. Welch. London, 1847. 8vo. Pamph., pp. 29. | Objects to a proposition to send convicts from the United Kingdom, whose term of punishment had expired, to New South Wales. |
| Wells ......... (1) | A Geographical Dictionary or Gazetteer of the Australian Colonies. By W. H. Wells. Sydney, 1848. 8vo. | A scarce and valuable book; gives correct information on the geography and topography of the Colony to the date of publication. |
| Wentworth... (3.4.5) - | A statistical, historical, and political description of the Colony of New South Wales. By W. C. Wentworth. London, 1820. 8vo. | Contains a useful and trustworthy account of the early history of New South Wales. The author was for many years one of the leading public men in the Colony, and the framer of its present Constitution. |
| Wentworth... (3 to 7) | A Statistical Account of the British Settlements in Australasia, including the Colonies of New South Wales and Van Diemen's Land. By W. C. Wentworth. 2 vols. 8vo. London, 1824. | This is a valuable work, as it affords authentic information as to the early settlement of the Colony, its exploration, products, and politics. |
| Wentworth... (4.5) | Public Funeral of the late William Charles Wentworth, Tuesday, 6th May, 1873. Sydney. 8vo. | "In the hearts of the people there was an earnest desire that the life-long services of Mr. Wentworth should be nationally recognized, and in both Houses of Parliament distinguished Members gave to this great public desire form and eloquent expression." |
| Westgarth .... (3.4.5) | Report, Commercial, Statistical, and General, of the District of Port Phillip, N. S. W., for the half-year ending 31st July, 1846. Melbourne. 8vo. Pamph. pp. 7. | Contains useful information on all subjects connected with the Colony. |
| Westgarth .... (3 to 6) | Australia Felix; or, a Historical and Descriptive Account of the Settlement of Port Phillip, New South Wales; with particulars of the manners and customs of the Aboriginal Natives. By W. Westgarth. Edinburgh, 1848. 8vo. | A chapter on the Legislature of New South Wales and the Administration of the Colonies; zoology and botany; establishment of the settlement at Port Phillip, now Melbourne, the capital of Victoria. |

| Mode of Reference. | Full Title, &c. | Remarks. |
|---|---|---|
| Wheelwright (4) | Sporting Sketches at Home and Abroad. By H. W. Wheelwright (The Old Bushman). London, 1866. 12mo. | Contains two chapters on hunting and sporting in Australia. |
| White ......... (3.4.5) | Journal of a Voyage to New South Wales, with 65 Plates of nondescript Animals, Plants, &c. By John White, Esq., Surgeon General to the Settlement. London, 1790. 4to. | Gives a very full and trustworthy account of the early settlement of the Colony, with interesting remarks on the fauna and flora. |
| Wilhelmi ...... (4) | Manners and Customs of the Australian Natives. By Charles Wilhelmi. Melbourne, 1862. 8vo. Pamph. pp. 43. | Specially relates to the Port Lincoln tribes, but is applicable in many of its details to the tribes of New South Wales. |
| Wilkes......... (4.5) | Narrative of the United States' Exploring Expedition during the years 1838–42. By Charles Wilkes, Admiral, U.S.N. Philadelphia, 1845. 5 vols. 4to. | That portion which refers to New South Wales gives a truthful description of Sydney and the adjoining country, manners of the Aborigines, &c. |
| Wills ......... (1.5) | A successful Expedition through the Interior of Australia, from Melbourne to the Gulf of Carpenteria. From the journals and letters of William John Wills. Edited by his father, W. Wills. London, 1863. 8vo. | Full of trustworthy geographical information. |
| Wilson ........ (1.5) | Narrative of a Voyage round the World, and description of British Settlements on the Coast of New Holland, &c. By T. B. Wilson, M.D. London, 1835. 8vo. | The remarks on New South Wales are very meagre. |
| Woods ......... (1.5) | A History of the Discovery and Exploration of Australia. By the Rev. J. E. T. Woods. London, 1865. 2 vols. 8vo. | This history has been brought down to the year 1863. It is well written, and accurate in its details. |
| Wool ......... (3) | Abstract of Evidence taken before the Select Committee of the House of Lords, appointed to take into consideration the state of the British Wool Trade. London, 1828. 8vo. Pamph. | Interesting, as showing at what an early date in the history of the Colony the superior quality of the wool was recognised in the English market; and also, the anticipation that New South Wales would prove a great wool-producing country. |
| Wool ......... (3) | Catalogue of Wools for the London International Exhibition of 1862, and for competition for Messrs. Mort & Co.'s Gold Medal. Sydney, 1862. Fol. | Gives the names of some of the principal wool-growers of New South Wales, with Jurors' awards on their produce. |
| Woolls......... (4.5) | A short account of the character and labours of the Rev. Samuel Marsden, formerly principal Chaplain of the Church of England in New South Wales. By W. Woolls. Parramatta, 1844. 12mo. | An account of early missionary efforts in New South Wales and New Zealand. For another account of Mr. Marsden see Wentworth's Statistical Account of British Settlements in Australasia, also Marsden. |

| Mode of Reference. | Full Title, &c. | Remarks. |
|---|---|---|
| Woolls......... (3) | A contribution to the Flora of Australia. By William Woolls, F.L.S. Sydney, 1867. 8vo. | A valuable addition to our knowledge of the Botany of New South Wales. |
| Woolls......... (3) | The progress of Botanical Discovery in Australia : a lecture by W. Woolls, F.L.S. Sydney, 1869. 12mo. Pamph. pp. 41. | Contains much information in reference to the Botanists of N. S. W., and the result of their researches. |
| Woore......... (1.4) | The Warragamba Water Scheme. By Thomas Woore. Sydney, 1872. 8vo. Pamph. pp. 19. | A project to supply Sydney with water from the Warragamba by gravitation |
| Woore......... (3.4) | Lectures on Railways, delivered at the Goulburn Mechanics' Institute, by Thos. Woore, Esq. Sydney, 1855. 12mo. Pamph. pp. 22. | A review of railway construction generally, with special reference to the extension of the line to Goulburn. |
| Woore......... (3.4) | Australian Railways and the Sydney University Magazine. By T. Woore. Sydney. (No date.) 8vo. Pamph. pp. 11. | A discussion as to the probable cost of a railway from Sydney to Goulburn, with particulars of cost of similar lines in other countries, etc. |
| Woore......... (1.4.) | Remarks on what New South Wales might become by introducing the light of science into it. By Thomas Woore. Sydney, 1876. 8vo. Pamph. pp. 19. Comments on Mr. Clark's Report on Water Supply to Sydney, New South Wales. By Thomas Woore. Sydney, 1877. 8vo. Pamph. pp. 12. | Refer principally to the question of Water Supply for Sydney; are opposed to the course recommended by Mr. Clark. (q.v.) |
| Wyndham ... (4.5) | The Impending Crisis. By George Wyndham. Maitland, 1847. 12mo. Pamph. pp. 12. | A chapter from Blackstone on property; applied by Mr. Wyndham to the discussion then before the public in reference to the tenure of squattages. |
| Wyndham ... (4.5) | A letter to Sir John Bull, Bart, upon the disposal of Crown Lands in the Colonies. By a Squatter (G. Wyndham). Sydney, 1847. 8vo. Pamph. pp. 15. | Advocates that grants of land should be made to all who improve it ; and that as America has been an outlet for European surplus population, so Australia should be to Asia. |
| Wyndham ... (4.5) | The Land Question.—Address of the President (John Wyndham, Esq.), of the Hunter River Agricultural Association. Maitland, September, 1873. Sydney, 1873. 8vo. Pamph. pp. 8. | This pamphlet endeavours to show that the payment for land under the present system is unjust, and proposes in lieu thereof that a gift in land be made over by the Crown to the squatters, who, with free selectors and others, should be forced to pay a land tax. |

Sydney : Thomas Richards, Government Printer.—1878.

www.ingramcontent.com/pod-product-compliance
Lightning Source LLC
Chambersburg PA
CBHW031759090426
42739CB00008B/1079